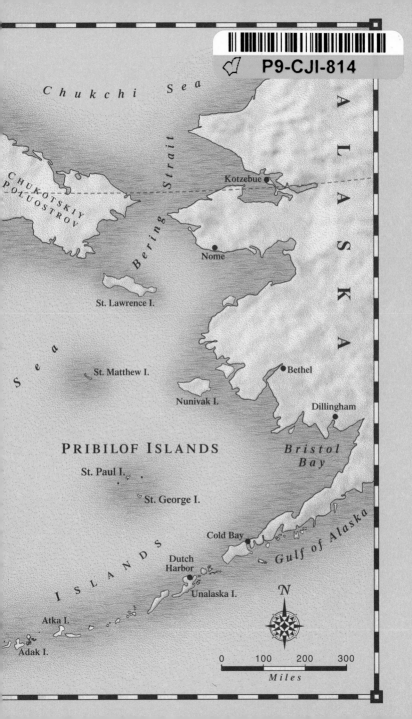

Seven Words for Wind

Seven Words for Wind

Essays and Field Notes
from Alaska's Pribilof Islands

SUMNER MACLEISH

 Epicenter Press
Fairbanks/Seattle

Epicenter Press Inc. is a regional press founded in Alaska, whose interests include but are not limited to the arts, history, environment, and diverse cultures and lifestyles of the North Pacific and high latitudes. We seek both the traditional and innovative in publishing quality nonfiction tradebooks, contemporary art and photography giftbooks, and destination travel guides emphasizing Alaska, Washington, Oregon, and California.

Editors: Valerie Griffith, Christine Ummel
Project Editor: B.G. Olson
Dust Jacket and Inside Design: Newman Design/Illustration
Maps: Rusty Nelson
Front Dust Jacket Photo: High cliffs and kittiwakes on
   St. George Island, Pribilofs. Photograph ©1996 Tim Thompson.
Back Dust Jacket Photo: Village on St. Paul Island.
   Photograph ©1996 Allen Prier/Alaska Stock Images.
Printer: Best Book Manufacturers

Library of Congress catalog card number: 97-075309

Text and interior photography © 1997 Sumner MacLeish

To order single copies of SEVEN WORDS FOR WIND, mail $16.95 plus $5 for Priority Mail shipping (Washington residents add $1.46 sales tax) to: Epicenter Press, Box 82368, Kenmore, WA 98028.

Booksellers: Retail discounts are available from our trade distributor, Graphic Arts Center Publishing™, Box 10306, Portland, OR 97210. Phone 800-452-3032.

First Printing, October 1997
10 9 8 7 6 5 4 3 2 1
Printed in Canada

For Leatha, Marissa,
and Ian Alexander
with love.

Contents

9 FOREWORD *by* B. G. OLSON

11 ACKNOWLEDGMENTS

13 MAP *of* ST. PAUL ISLAND

15 Slatux̂
   A sequence of winds, to blow hard

31 Slachxidaasaadagûlux
   A very strong storm

49 Slam Kadiigux̂taa
   A contrary wind

67 Alaĝulix
   To go into the sea

91 Asxi-lix
   To go against the wind

111 Qutaxt
   Blowing up from land

131 Qag, Agaagalix̂
   East wind, west wind

147 Chax̂atax̂
   An offshore wind

153 FURTHER READING

159 AUTHOR'S NOTE

Foreword

On a fall morning in 1993, I stood by my living room window on St. Paul Island waiting for my neighbor Sumner MacLeish and her young son, Ian, to drop by for tea and a book-planning session.

The wind was steady at 45 knots with gusts to 65, violently hurling waves and spray over the thirty-foot breakwater of the harbor and smashing them high on the black cliff of Tolstoi Point. The island sparkled in bright sun as my house moaned and rattled in the gale. With Ian in her arms, Sumner stepped from her door into the wind and was blown backwards repeatedly. Finally she drove the thirty yards to my house. When she left two hours later, the wind was calm, and the dying grass and wildflowers were glistening with the dampness of heavy fog and light mist that obliterated the sun.

The weather that day was not an anomaly. Lives on this remote, treeless island are sculpted by weather, as is the island itself. High winds, swirling fog, thick mists, winter ice packs, blizzards—sudden, erratic change. The volatile, capricious weather in this "cradle of storms" not only creates the patterns and tone of life on the island, but also helps mold the weather of the entire North American continent.

Fourteen miles long and eight wide, the volcanic island is home to a roving reindeer herd, and the breeding grounds and summer home for almost a million fur seals and hundreds of thousands of cliff-dwelling seabirds.

Its remote location—in the Bering Sea, 200 miles north of Dutch Harbor and 770 miles southwest of

Anchorage—also unsparingly impacts the daily lives and culture of St. Paul's 600 Aleut residents, the earth's largest Aleut population. Aleuts were brought to St. Paul from the Aleutian Islands by Russians as "slaves of the seal harvest" in 1786. They remained wards of the United States government after the purchase of Alaska in 1867, and through Alaska's Statehood in 1959, until the Alaska Native Claims Settlement Act was passed in 1971.

Writer Sumner MacLeish knows and loves the island and its people. Born in Boston in a literary family, she grew up in London and Washington, D.C. She has worked in communications as a reporter and photographer for two decades, produced two documentaries for National Public Radio, and has been a commentator for Alaska Public Radio.

In 1984, while covering the Democratic National Convention in San Francisco, Sumner heard about the controversy over commercial sealing in the Pribilofs. She contacted a young Aleut leader, Larry Merculieff, from St. Paul Island, and spent the next year working on a documentary about the Pribilovians. Over the next four years she returned to fish commercially with Merculieff. In 1990 they married and Sumner moved to the island.

Sumner is distinctively qualified to write about the island. She has been both an observer and a participant of the island's culture and daily life. She loves the wind, the storms and sudden changes, the pace of life, and the people.

Seven Words for Wind is thoughtful and provocative literature. Sumner's magical sentences and brilliant images create a deeply moving portrayal of an island and a proud people in transition, striving to preserve a culture and way of life in a remote corner of the world. Hers is the voice of an important young writer.

B. G. Olson
St. Paul Island, Alaska

Acknowledgments

Many people contributed to the writing of this book. My deepest appreciation: to Diana Chapin MacLeish for her fierce intelligence, excellent editorial skills, and gentle heart; to Rod MacLeish for his love of knowledge and extraordinary gift with language; to Isabel Ann Kip for asking all the right questions and for being luminous in the dark; to Ilarion Paul Merculieff for his steadfast support, his commitment to conservation, and his visionary work in bringing together people and ideas; to Stefanida Oustigoff for her love and for teaching me so much; to Isolde Chapin for her great understanding and allegiance; to Eric MacLeish for always challenging me and for his brilliant advocacy of the rights of others; to Rinna Merculieff for her dedication to helping others, her independence of spirit, and her unparalleled companionship while fishing; to Piama Merculief for her wondrous friendship and life-giving sense of humor; to Phyllis Anne Swetzoff for her powers of observation, her unfailing energy, and for being a profoundly involved Pribilovian; to Ian Alexander's *yaayaĝs* Simeon Swetzoff Jr., John R. Merculieff, Mike Zacharof, Greg Fratis, and Larry Chapman, and to *tuutkaĝs* Georgia Paulus, Pauline Rukovishnikoff, and Julie Shane for the warmth of their friendship; to Susanne Swibold and Helen Corbett for their critical thinking, uncompromising integrity, and dedicated work on behalf of Aleuts everywhere; and to Misha Flint for his exceptional engagement with life and his absolute love of the sea.

This book was more accident than planned project and it was only through the encouragement, persistence, and patience of B. G. Olson and Kent Sturgis of Epicenter Press that it became a book. My great thanks to them and to editors Christine Ummel and Valerie Griffith for their straight talk, clear thinking, and sharp attention to detail.

A portion of the author's royalties from this book will go toward funding research of the Pribilof Islands marine ecosystem and the establishment of educational research centers on the Pribilof Islands and Komandorskiye Ostrova.

St. Paul Island

Bering Sea

Northeast Point

Sea Lion Point

North Point

Tasmania

North Hill

Big Lake

Rush Hill

Crater Hill

High Bluffs

Cone Hill

Bogoslov

Polovina

Airport

Southwest Point

USCG Loran Station

U.S. Weather Service

Zapadni Point

Diamond Hill

Lukanin Bay

Tolstoi Point

Salt Lagoon

Village

Kitovi Point

Reef Point

Lookout Rock

Sea Lion Rock

N

0 1 2 3 4 5

Miles

Major Seal Rookeries

Slatux̂

A sequence of winds, to blow hard

ALEUTS HAVE at least seven words for wind, many of which refer to strength. Day after day, night after night, and sometimes for weeks on end, the wind pushes across hundreds of miles of open water, across this small plate of land in the Bering Sea, and through our village on St. Paul Island. Once I asked a visiting priest about death as we stood on a bluff watching gusts of air darken the water. "The body dies, decays," he said, turning to me, then smiling. "But the soul is energy." For years after that I imagined the wind gathering up the island's souls as it swept over us, absorbing even the frailest before scattering their luminous energy, that colorless light, towards Russia, the Arctic, or south to the Amundsen Sea.

At fifty-seven degrees latitude, 770 miles west of Anchorage, and 200 miles north of the Aleutian Chain, the Pribilof Islands rise from the shallow continental shelf to surface just above the Bering Sea. It is a region noted as much for its turbulent weather as it is for its exceptional wildlife. Five small islands and the marine ecosystem surrounding them support extraordinary concentrations of marine mammals, seabirds, fish, and shellfish. Alternately graced and battered by oceanic and atmospheric events, winters can stretch over six months. Summers flare abruptly like intense storms bearing light and a dazzling fecundity: over a million northern fur seals, two million seabirds, and fantastic populations of fish migrate to the Pribilofs each year to breed, bear young, and feed in the rich waters around them.

The two largest islands, St. Paul and St.
George, are home to about 750 Aleuts, Alaska
Natives whose ancestors settled along the
southern edge of the Bering Land Bridge some
eight to ten thousand years ago. It is a landscape of immense contrast and complexity, a
place of solitude and conflict, mischief and
advantage, a work in progress influenced as
much by the forces of nature as by the force of
man. Named now for the Russian sea navigator
Gerrassium Pribylov, who came upon the
islands searching for fur seals two hundred
years ago, the Aleuts have long known the
Pribilofs as *Tanax̂ Amix̂*, "Land of Mother's
Uncle," and by that name conveyed their
reverence for this place and the life it supports.

The wind out here can be sudden and fierce
like thunder or long and running like a great
strong river deep in the ocean. Yet those who
live and work in this area lean toward under-
statement in the face of such operatic behavior.
Villagers rarely remark on the wind except in
reference to how it may affect fishing or hunt-

ing plans. Crab fishermen, talking back and forth on their radios, refer to gales as "rock 'n roll" weather even as they maneuver their boats closer to shore. A good blow can bring them in to anchor while winter ducks, like scoters, eiders, harlequins, and oldsquaws, ride the same heaving waves in thin, unsinkable bracelets.

Given adequate warning of a storm, commercial fishing boats and processing ships in the Pribilof region will head for the lee side of our island to wait out the weather. One night I counted eighty-three of them beyond the breakwater, anchored up but rocking and rolling in the chop, engines roaring, banks of blinding halogen lights illuminating the water and nearby headlands. It looked as though a glittering city had suddenly risen beside the village. Not Atlantis by any stretch, the golden age restored, Zeus's drowning of a continent of sinners undone. This was big machinery. It was big money, big politics, and big pollution. We live like this now on what were once truly remote, wild islands: pushed up against the present, rubbing shoulders with steel and greed.

A great storm, *slachxidamulux iĝanaasaadaa*, passes. The boats head out again and the color of the water changes, the winter sun emerges white as the moon, and the sea's minute plants and animals settle into darker places. On the island we comb the beaches for anything the wind and sea may have brought or uncovered: a mammoth's stone-like tooth or long ivory tusk, neon-colored fishing buoys, the wing of a bird, scalloping feathers and bone.

For awhile, we forget our troubled relation-ship with the Bering Sea fishing fleet, forget our concern over not having forged a more diverse and conservation-based economy, a concern that settles like a net over our intent. For awhile, we are just six hundred people heading into another winter. Land animals— mother, sister, father, and son, among the fox, reindeer, lemmings, and winged strangers blown in from the storm.

The fire of autumn, of grasses gone gold during long, brilliant days under a cerulean sky, has passed and the tundra, washed by *slatux̂*, a sequence of winds, lies flat along the headlands

and the open plains of the island. Winter has
driven huge glaucous gulls and small foxes into
the village where they scavenge for food, com-
peting with feral and recently abandoned cats.
A certain frontier civility among the animals
grows apparent in the wide corridors between
our homes as hungry foxes and starving cats
walk within inches of one another without
striking out. Only the gulls remain unruly, their
keen cries over the rumor of food mingling
with the cats' mews until, like voices in a
dream, it is hard to tell who is who.

Inside the house, the weather forecast on
the radio repeats quietly, endlessly through the
day. We are inordinately interested in the
weather, and in the ironic, expensive infrastructure particular to the most distant Alaskan
outposts, there is a fully staffed U.S. Weather
Bureau just outside the village. Special bulle-
tins, speaking to our concerns, are issued under
certain conditions: "There is a high wind
warning out this morning. Winds to seventy
knots with higher gusts. Residents are advised
to keep small children inside today." And later:

"High winds continue this afternoon. Residents are advised to watch out for flying debris."

The meteorologists know us well. Not much deters people here from going about as they usually do—even a hard wind, *slaĝuuchxuzax̂*, is a backdrop, part of the winter canvas we lean into as we go about our business. Power lines and telephone cables are buried underground. Houses are built with double-door storm entrances. Vehicles are parked into the wind so their doors won't snap off when opened. The old grader keeps up with drifting snow and the new sand truck works well on icy, windburned roads. But we do watch out for our children and we keep an eye out for flying debris.

The fiercest storm I've seen, *slachxidaasaadaĝulux*, came through a long November night with a persistence and power that tore at roofs, pounded walls, shattered windows and any disbelief I may have had in the thunderous rage of Aeolus. When a window exploded into our bedroom at midnight, my husband Larry and I spent an hour boarding it up. When the entire bedroom began to shake, we decided to sleep in the living room. But there, a loosened strip of sheet metal roofing slapped, smashed, and arced into the night just above a large window. Another roof sheet sliced back and forth outside between our house and that of our nearest neighbor. Watching it, I saw my pickup truck dancing— the frame moving up and down, the large tires pulled between gravity and weightlessness. We gave up the idea of sleep, waited for daylight, felt the house shudder, shift, and moan as if made alive by the roaring wind. In the morning, the village looked as if it had been sandblasted. Fourteen fishing boats in the region had been abandoned.

Remarkably, there were no deaths on land or at sea. Still, the storm stayed with me in unexpected ways. Ten hours of 70- to 100-mph winds left me wondering whether we belong out here with our clapboard houses, HUD homes, high-tech boats, and incautious ways. Up until two hundred years ago, Aleuts lived in *baraabarax̂*, individual and communal dwellings dug into the earth, so that the wind swept over them as over so many other hills. Their traditional sea kayaks, the most sophisticated among maritime cultures, had as many as sixty small animal bones strategically inserted into the framework as joints so that every part of the *iqyaĵ* was in motion as it moved across the sea. Such ingenious craftsmanship, learned over thousands of years, was ignored by the succession of more "civilized" people, people who rushed in from the west and then from the east with only one thing in mind—money.

Between then and now, the Aleut story is similar to those of indigenous people around the world. The *baraabaraĵ* and the sea kayaks are long gone, as is much of the Aleuts' considerable knowledge about navigation, medicine, the ways of animals, of nature, survival, and adaptation. Their language, full of abrupt and long vowels, of *uxs* and *udthas* and guttural Rs, mixed dialects, words borrowed from Russian, and untranslatable expressions, will never again be commonly spoken after my mother-in-law's generation is gone. There is a growing movement among the Aleuts now to hold onto the practices that help define and distinguish their culture, to learn about and reclaim vanishing traditions, to anchor themselves as their ancestors did so successfully. Yet the November storm that swept over us a few years ago seemed to me a reckoning of sorts, evidence of things lost and unrecoverable when, with the passage of time, we fail to bring any of the past forward.

My willful tendency to explore under any conditions, to head out into a storm, prompted my husband to remind me about the disorienting effects of wind and snow and to advise me against straying far from the village in rough winter weather. Housebound during blizzards, I watched shape-shifting forms appear and disappear: huge sheets of muslin swept across the tundra, herds of ghost animals rushed toward the sea. Often, however, there was no snow or rain with the wind. One clear night during a strong blow I drove up onto Diamond Hill. For a long time I lay in the bed of my

pickup truck in a cathedral of stars, mesmerized
by the universe, the darkness, and the muffled
sound of the wind through my parka. What
caught me off guard and held me there in the
cold night was its unexpected familiarity. Here
was the very landscape I had seen and heard,
through the technology of ultrasound, inside
my own body just before my son was born: the
bits of vernix floating up from his body like
stars against the blackness of my womb, the
near, rushing sound of blood and air from my
heart and lungs all around him.

Once I heard wind and thought of death
and the gathering up of souls. Now I hear wind
as a voice across the earth. My mother reminds
me that *anima*, the Latin word for soul, comes
from *anemos*, the Greek word for wind: I think,
it is no loose magic, this circle of knowledge, no
primitive alchemy. It is matter made metaphysical, the narrative to which we turn and
return, looking for clues across a landscape as
dark as it is brilliant.

Field Notes

I first came
to St. Paul
Island in 1984
to produce a
documentary
about the Pribilovians and the end of commercial sealing. I arrived knowing little, least
of all that my own life would soon change
direction though the course was true: toward
nature, wildness, and space. The documentary
was made, friendships followed, one unexpect-
edly deepening into love so that six years
later I moved to the island, married Ilarion
Paul Merculieff in the small Orthodox church,
and settled into this wheel-like landscape
where the sky falls into the water and the
water rises into the sky.

It's difficult to say what bound me to this
place. Perhaps it was the right mix of solitude—that most necessary freedom—and
companionship. Maybe it was the chance to lose
myself in the detail and drama of weather and

wildlife—to be farther away and yet closer to
the things that seemed, increasingly, important.

I put away all my photographic and recording equipment, bought watercolors and brushes,
went from reading several newspapers a day and
listening to every hour's news to caring
mostly for the new essentials: the marine forecast, a bi-monthly newspaper from the Aleutian
Chain, rumors, poetry, and the cogent, irrever-
ent thoughts of family, neighbors, and friends.

I cut off and dried the fine-toothed beaks
and lattice-veined webbed feet of the ducks my
husband hunted and killed, once, to his cha-
grin, mounting them in a gilded wood frame the
way trophy hunters grotesquely display their
kills. I chased reckless fishermen who raced
through the village on rented all-terrain
vehicles, cornered them at the dock, and read
them the riot act. I was alarmingly eager to
go on hazardous search and rescue trips as an
emergency medical technician, to climb up rope
ladders onto foreign trawlers in the middle of
the night.

I spoke with a directness that was not

entirely appropriate. It wasn't that I spoke
too much, but that I was straightforward.
Though its glacial pace often exasperated me,
I learned to appreciate the value of circui-
tous talk, the way criticism or anger can be
deflected, the way a point can be made through
the unfolding of conversation.

Far from feeling isolated and off the
beaten track, I felt at The Center, my attention riveted by the day-long approach of a
storm from the south, or a close encounter
with a fox, the evidence of design everywhere,
and everywhere the design undone, mutating,
glimpsed, and gone. Each twist of nature had
the effect of loosening the accumulated perceptions of life I'd held and untying the
knots of my ordinary knowledge.

I knew I was not alone in this feeling,
that there were others whose experiences on
the island transcended some threshold, drew
and held them close and would not let them go.
Many Aleuts expressed similar thoughts, and of
course for them the pull was all the stronger
as this was home, physically, culturally,
spiritually. For some villagers it was a

bittersweet thing, as such ties to a homeland
often prove: the past appearing in brief
gestures of light through a familiar window,
the smell in a camphouse, the sound of someone
in the kitchen but otherwise lost in the
discontinuous, preoccupied present.

Living in a wild and beautiful place I
learned that it is both necessary and exces-
sive to give one's weight completely to
whatever is at hand: the sound of night; of
electricity just before it goes out; the sight
of least auklets sweeping off the breakwater
as if they were one fluid hand of a dancer
gesturing toward the sea; the way pre-dawn
cold burns your eyes as you lie on a shelf of
ice watching winter ducks cross a dark half-
moon of open water. I learned that a seemingly
flawed life can be deeply privileged; that
nature and her creatures live in a more reasonable, more complex world than I may ever know.

And I learned to taste things I never would
have thought to try: another person's shame,
for instance, and the wet, rolling wind off
the sea.

Slachxidaasaadagûlux

A very strong storm

"WE WERE BROUGHT UP to believe the white man had the answers," said my sister-in-law. "Not to trust our own people." As a child, Rinna Merculieff assimilated the spoken and unspoken beliefs of her parents and other Aleuts living in a contemptuous and frequently humiliating atmosphere. The house she grew up in was inspected weekly for cleanliness by a white man wearing a white glove. Canned and even wild foods were tightly rationed; the freshest fruit came from a nearby dump where

Rinna and other children found oranges and
apples sometimes discarded by the white people.
At night she slept, along with her brothers and
sister, under a thin army blanket in a cement
house heated by a small kitchen stove. The
electricity was turned off at ten o'clock.

For thousands of years the only human
presence on the Pribilof Islands was that of the
Native hunter or hunting party in search of
food or shelter during a storm. Then, two
hundred years ago, trouble arrived in the form
of *promyshlennikis*—fur traders from Russia's
Far East. Their thirty-year presence on the
Aleutian Chain had already decimated the
Aleut people as village after village was
"taken," the inhabitants murdered, forced into
slavery, left dead or dying from the diseases
brought by white men. It was the abundant sea
otter population and their prized fur the
promyshlennikis had been after and then pur-
sued until they were gone. The traders then
looked toward the fur seals which migrated
through the chain's many passes each spring

and fall. Sixty Siberian trading companies spent ten years searching the North Pacific and Bering Sea for the land base of this great seal herd. Gerrassium Pribylov was the chief navigator for the largest of these trading companies and it was his ship, the *St. George*, that eventually ran aground in thick fog on one of the seal islands. It was June 25, 1786. The first human settlements on the two largest islands were soon established as the *promyshlennikis* forcibly brought Aleuts north to kill, skin, and package the seal pelts.

For a hundred years, hundreds of thousands of fur seals were killed on the Pribilofs as they returned each summer to mate and bear their young. The seal's dense fur—300,000 hairs per square inch—provided precious warmth to those wealthy enough to afford the coats and other clothing fashioned from their pelts. The unregulated killing of fur seals seemed matched only by the intemperate demand for their skins as their reputation spread west across the world's largest continent, through Europe, eventually crossing the Atlantic to come full circle to North America.

By the 1860s the Pribilof fur seal population had been greatly diminished by a century of unrestrained killing. The Russian Empire's human and financial resources had been strained by the Crimean War, and further colonization of North America seemed improbable. So it was that in 1867, the Tsarist government of Russia signed a treaty of cessation with America, transferring, on paper, the right to govern Alaska and its people to the United States for $7.2 million. Ratification of the treaty was barely approved by a Congress grappling with more pressing issues than the acquisition of a territory far, far away.

The prodigious subterranean reserves of Alaska—from the thick, unctuous fields of oil, to the mountains of silver white metallic molybdenum, and the many elements and minerals in between—could not even have been imagined in the late 1800s. But the treaty would increase America's land mass by almost 50 percent and would proffer a geographical and political statement to westward-expanding

Canada. And, it was rumored, there was "gold" out on those seal islands. By one vote more than the two-thirds required for passage, the United States Congress ratified the treaty on June 20, 1867.

Another hundred years of captive Aleut labor and seal killing followed under the jurisdiction of the U.S. Department of Treasury and, later, the U.S. Department of Commerce. Revenue from this commercial seal harvest quickly repaid the original cost of Alaska and would continue to generate millions of dollars for the country. A crude conservation plan to maintain a maximum sustainable yield of fur seals emerged by trial and error. As had been the case with the Russian Empire, the principal aim of the United States government was profitable management of the seal herd. "Managing" the Aleut people forced to remain on St. Paul and St. George to perform the labor was secondary, based largely on their capacity to work. Supervised by a series of federal managers sent to oversee the seal harvest, the Pribilovians lived under often arbitrary and autocratic regulations.

As a teenager, Piama Gromoff, Rinna Merculieff's best friend, viewed the government clinic on St. Paul Island as more menacing than comforting. Capricious medical decrees, such as the circumcision of all boys up to six years of age, were issued by the government doctor. Teeth were pulled without Novocain. Piama's twelve-year-old brother was taken by force to the clinic after the doctor decided the tonsils of all village children should be removed. When her brother did not come home, their mother went to the clinic. She was told that her son was not well enough to come home. She was told that she could not see her son. Matushka Elizabeth, wife of the Reverend Elary Gromoff, was a gentle, dignified woman who persisted, returning to the clinic every day. After a week, the doctor let her see her son. By then, he was so ill from infection following the tonsillectomy that his mother barely recognized him. He died the next day.

Piama and Rinna are my age. We are close friends now with children of our own and it is

difficult to distance myself from their child-
hood experiences—or from those of my
husband, my mother-in-law, and other friends
with similar stories. Knowing them, loving
them, I find their grace, persistent humor, and
considerable accomplishments reminders of
the soundness and sanctity of the human spirit
and of their heritage.

In the end, nothing excuses the egregious
manner in which the Aleuts were treated. It is
difficult to convey the profound cultural and
spiritual destruction that swept through this
ancient, accomplished maritime society like
some malevolent two-hundred-year storm. Yet
the evidence of its passage and the broad, dark
wake of its path are everywhere.

"I don't hate the white man," Gabriel
Stepetin told me once. "But I don't trust him. I
never will. Not even you." He smiled and
laughed softly, taking my hand in his strong,
round hands but not looking at me. I, too,
looked away, around his living room at the icons
and the photographs, the set of World Book

Encyclopedias, the large framed picture of John F. Kennedy deep in thought. Gabe Stepetin was one of several renowned Pribilovian leaders during the late 1940s, 1950s, and 1960s whose persuasive, eloquent voice addressed political independence and human rights issues before numerous congressional committees and the U.N. Human Rights Commission.

Gabe spoke when others could not, found words that conveyed the dignity, intelligence, and knowledge of his people, pointed out the many grave injustices they had suffered without giving in to anger or bitterness. Though he died several years ago, his voice remains the voice of a generation, of the elders still living on St. Paul and St. George. Among those I know, as varied as they are in temperament and personality, there seems an almost uniform absence of ill feelings about the past. Most speak matter-of-factly about the hardships they endured. They are far more inclined to talk about the good times, to recount with typical self-effacement some of the funny things that happened, often as a

result of their deft acts of rebellion against government regulations. Among this oldest generation there is a profound connection to each other, an appreciation of the simplest pleasures, and an enduring capacity to amuse and be amused by life.

Many of these characteristics—resiliency, wry humor, and a sense of community—are equally evident in the next generation. But among my peers there is also anger: anger as an almost involuntary reaction, anger turned inward like a knife, or, as often, turned against each other. Alcoholism, divorce, and domestic violence plague many families. Deep personal and political rifts can escalate suddenly when flamed by exhaustion, frustration, or booze.

One woman ominously shadowed my every move for twenty-four hours after our husbands clashed at a meeting.

Still, my husband Larry and a handful of other leaders have lived lifted by flashing opportunities to set things right. Debbie Bourdukovsky has turned her ancestral research into a "living spirit" program that teaches young children and teenagers everything from the practical to the spiritual traditions of the Aleuts. Mike Swetzoff, Ron Philemonoff, Greg Fratis, Julie Shane, and others have transformed a day-boat fish processing shop into a multimillion-dollar high-tech operation that makes St. Paul a major player in the international fisheries market. Larry, John R. Merculief, and Mike Zacharov have made countless trips between St. Paul and Washington, D.C., to address subsistence, conservation, and resource management issues. And because of their exposure to and experience with the outside world, these Pribilovians live in a borderland, watching, wary, working to find a balance between their traditional ways and

evolving needs, to deflect what many regard as
the influence of a larger machine bent on
homogenizing everything in its path.

A true appreciation of cultural diversity, let
alone a tolerance for it, is not high on most
people's list despite the talk, despite the often
altruistic, even heroic efforts of some to make it
so. Often there is an absence of cross-cultural
understanding. More often there is misinfor-
mation, assumption, and arrogance of each
toward the other. Many of my Aleut friends are
race-conscious and speak of an underlying
suspicion that white people are generally insen-
sitive, materialistic, linear-thinking, overly
talkative urban dwellers out of touch with the
natural world. Some outsiders, I have found,
are equally contemptuous of the Aleuts, insist-
ing they have no culture, no right to kill seals
for food, no valid quarrel with history. Such
sentiments exist the way fault lines exist below
the most benign landscape.

There is considerable concern among my
peers about the future of the island and the
future of their children: in a community

plagued by the same social and environmental
ills of most communities, parents wonder how
their kids will find their way to adulthood and
whether they will want to come home, whether
they should come home, and what will be here
if they return. Will their children ever know
how accomplished their ancestors were? Would
they be surprised by their extensive medical
knowledge noted, for example, in a 1949 issue
of *The New England Journal of Medicine* and
numerous ethnographic publications? Or by
their superior celestial navigational skills that
allowed them to travel hundreds, even thousands of miles across open water to destinations
such as those now named Barrow, the
Komandorskiye, and the Hawaiian Islands?
Will their children take *their* children to the
Smithsonian's archives to handle the hundreds
of small, delicate carvings lying in storage
drawers, to touch the waterproof bird-skin
parkas that have been preserved, to wonder at
the ancient bentwood hunting hats carrying
centuries-old sea lion whiskers and a belief in
gods? Is it too much to ask for a benevolent

undertow that might pull their children back in time and then release them today with some sense of connection so that new pickup trucks and television and even computers are seen more clearly for what they are: things, of some value but of no profound substance, inorganic tricksters to be wary of in the broader pursuit of life? It is difficult to know.

It may be dramatic but it is not an over-statement that everything out here—the human animals and the marine mammals, the fish, the birds, and the health of the sea—all are at stake in the reconciliation of traditional conservation and the progressive disorder of man's misman-agement. The finned, flippered, and winged creatures are floundering in depleted waters while our own children are being hurtled into adulthood like chips beaten off a rock. The Pribilovians, like bitter, divorcing parents, argue among themselves over the custody of their future. On the horizon, countries negoti-ate treaties, rearrange borders, and claim sovereignty over things that cannot be owned and that are no longer negotiable. We believe we glimpse something greater, something more profound, but fear Rainer Maria Rilke was right, that "the future enters into us, in order to transform itself in us, long before it happens."

Field Notes

For over a year I was periodically obsessed with a small white hut located at the intersection of roads between "downtown" and "uptown." The hut, which opened like a market stall, was built by an "Outsider" who had recently moved to the island and wanted, among other things, to sell fireworks. The booth opened on an irregular schedule and proved a magnet for village kids—five-year-olds and fifteen-year-olds who frequently set off everything from sparklers to cherry bombs as soon as they were bought. I felt the entire venture was unsafe at best, lethal at worst. But the local authorities did not agree and had given the fireworks man a permit. The police agreed but had no legal recourse to close it down. Some of my friends and neighbors agreed but most, frankly, thought there were bigger fish to fry.

The white stall stayed. Open for perhaps a

total of eight weeks out of fifty-two, it sat center stage at the busiest crossroads on the island for almost two years. I dug out my cameras and photographed it whenever my obsession surged. I spoke to every influential person I knew, from elders to my husband (who was the city manager), but every effort I made was met with indifference. In a place where calamities, real and imagined, occur on a regular basis, no one shared my urgent sentiments that this hazardous structure should come down. My frustration came in spurts but was sufficiently tended so that, in time, the fireworks hut seemed an incongruous metaphor: of the damage wrought by the reckless acts of white men, and of the harm allowed by those unable or unwilling to respond. In short, I was vexed with everyone.

Two winters after the stall was built, one of the underground outfall lines from the fish plant to the sea broke. It was the height of the opilio crab season, with thousands of pounds of shellfish being processed every day. Economic disaster was a possibility. The line had to be fixed, even though the ground was frozen, even though a great storm was building, then blowing

until all visibility, day after day, was lost in
the wind, snow, and blistering cold. The public
works crew, a handful of seasoned men, bundled
up in clothes, doubled their shifts, and opened
up the road between the "downtown" fish plant
and east landing with jackhammers, sledgeham-
mers, and pickaxes. Nothing less than open-heart
surgery, I thought. By the fifth day the crew,
working beneath a huge halogen construction
light, had reached the intersection where the
fireworks stall stood. My father-in-law Peter
mentioned this coming back from the store one
morning. "Public works crew looks like space men
working on the moon down there," he said, gesturing toward their location.

After Peter left I drove down to the work
site. The light illuminated enough of the scene
for me to see the crew had torn down the fireworks stall to get at the outfall line.
Redemption comes in many forms. Though it took
several more days of unrelieved work in a bliz-
zard, the village was saved from the potentially
ruinous shutdown of the fish plant; and though I
appeared inexplicably giddy while the crisis
continued, the true madness in me was gone.

Slam Kadiigux̂taa

A contrary wind

T HE DAYS and nights turn slowly, one stretching into the other. Outside, somewhere between winter and spring, the pale earth and cold sea touch the lip of a darkening sky. There is a stillness everywhere, a no-sound-even-from-the-birds stillness across the dull tundra, the slack water, the unremarkable horizon. In the village there is a different stillness as if people had lost their voices and the children were gone though, of course, they are not. They are all there in school and blue at night in front of the tube.

With the bar closed, only the foxes work the cold evening air.

By the third week of Lent few of us are moving—except to work and school—even fewer to church services every morning and evening. The men are restless. Unable to hunt, their thoughts shadow the sea lions' course along the eastern shore, north to south, south to north below Lookout Rock towards Kitovi Point, across Lukanin Bay, past the Polovina cliff rookeries and off the long, curving coast where the dark sand dunes sweep north to Sea Lion Point. Even villagers who haven't been to church in years seem bound by this seven-week covenant of prayer and penitence, though who knows what goes on behind closed doors or within bruised hearts.

"Weather would be warmer if people went to church," says Stefanida Oustigoff, my mother-in-law, her voice level. There was no heat in church this morning as I stood near her. The few of us there looked like ghosts, spirit breath curling before us in the long blocks of daylight. Father George asked, "Grant us the purity of faith and the beauty of soul," as he walked towards the iconostasis, but I could not see his breath as he spoke, only the disturbed clouds of incense whirling around him.

Grant us the purity of faith and the beauty of soul. I come to this small church where I was baptized and married for such simple, eloquent prayers, for the beauty of this plain church dressed, as for a ball, with icons from all over the world, bright plastic flowers, white candles, gold crosses, and chalices beneath its domed roof. Here the cosmos is clearly defined: we stand in the narthex, representing earth, facing the iconostasis—a broad floor-to-ceiling wall— behind which is heaven, or the sanctuary. I come for the hours of quiet, for the girlish whispering with Piama, and for the known, uneven voices of the a capella choir. I feel comfort and joy in the company of those around me, these people I know, the women standing on the left, the men on the right, the babies gently folded into neighboring arms, the children back and forth between mothers and fathers, *kruusnax̂s* (godparents), *aachax̂s* (mentors), *tuutkax̂s* (aunties), and *yaayax̂s* (uncles). I come for the sound of Slavonic and the Russian-Aleut loan-words. And I come out of curiosity—not for the church, as the church is familiar, but out of curiosity about God in whom I believe and don't believe.

How, then, do I understand the stillness outside? How to explain the way we speak of evil here as routinely as we speak of the weather? In what context—religious, spiritual, metaphysical—do I come to terms with countless "Bulgakovian" incidents, commonplace events that turn inexplicable, mysterious, veiled?

Like the fox.

Walking out along the Reef Point headlands one spring morning, I stopped to look over the arctic ice pack several hundred yards off shore. For weeks I had watched as it loomed on the horizon like a huge drifting continent. That morning it surrounded the island. The open water between the ice and shore was the color of dark sapphire, a fluid, fractured jewel in the bright sunlight. Kneeling down on top of a bluff to watch a handful of scoters on the

water, I suddenly noticed a fox near me. Dead, though hard to tell at first as she was partially curled up, as if settling into sleep. The dark fur on her head moved gently in the breeze, a soft brown face with a white blaze between her closed eyes. The rest of her body was still, the thick winter coat frozen and splayed by a long-gone wind. I lay close to her, listening to the sea, wondering how she had died.

I walked out to see her every morning for the next few days and each day she looked more a part of the frozen cliff until only the tip of an ear showed beneath the hard-packed snow. One night I dreamed I was falling from the same cliff, my heart racing, the dead fox slipping off the ledge above, tumbling toward me, into me, both of us into the sea.

The next day the dead fox was gone. In her place, in the same spot, was another fox, this one very much alive, sitting on the bluff looking out across the ice pack. As I approached, the fox turned, stared, and then trotted off. I dug into the snow with the heels of my boots, kicked it away until I hit the hard earth, knelt and swept my arms around, crept on my stomach to the edge of the cliff, and saw only what I'd seen before: the well-marked ledges, the rocks and water below. The dead fox was gone.

Which was the dream, which was real: the fox or the dream? Was this the kind of incident Aleuts might regard as one of many natural/ spiritual/atomic connections in life: waking, dreaming, animal to animal?

Grant us the purity of faith in all we experience. It is these ordinary matters turned curious— Stefanida's observation of the reciprocity between church attendance and the weather— and similar shifts in perspective that speak to other ways of "knowing" the world. I value this even though I lack my husband's and many of my friends' acceptance of the extraordinary as commonplace. I cannot share their refuge in the cumulative history of observation, custom, and experience that is their culture. And I do not understand the dual faith in traditional tribal explanations of spiritual and physical life and in the God-as-the-Orthodox-Church-presents-Him view of such things.

Holy water here is holy water. Glass jars filled with tap water and blessed by the priest are found in most homes and even in, especially in, the most remote camphouses around the island where spirits seem to feel more free to knock about. Every room in every house in the village is physically blessed with fresh holy water twice a year following Russian Christmas and Easter. Every fishing boat is brought to the blessing of the fleet, where prayers led by the priest accompany the spattering of a holy water cross across each hull. Most fishermen turn to the east and make the sign of the cross when they leave the harbor for a sea governed by wind, temperature, currents, and—who am I to say?—possibly the hand of God.

It's true that I am the one who barely got through our Orthodox marriage without resisting the opportunity to discuss a point or two mid-ceremony. For this is my heritage, the innate questioning of the absolute, of the given. It is the defining line I trip over, again and again.

Still, I am not as far from this challenge as my inheritance might imply. I have heard the unmistakable rapping—loud and territorial—on the door of an empty camphouse from which I've walked away after a night of believing, and not believing, I was in the company of spirits. I have lived through the brooding, ominous events that followed our lives after my husband shot but did not kill a powerful dark bird blown in by a storm, a marauder no other villager would dare approach because of its potent reputation. I have appreciated Some Presence in the miracle of a child growing inside me. Am I so different then?

Somewhere in the wide lava tubes that crisscross the island beneath the tundra lives a creature villagers call *Tayaĝunaax̂*—"Outside Man"—a man-like figure covered with fur. Few

here doubt his existence. My sister-in-law
Rinna vividly remembers Tayaĝunaax̂'s hairy
face looking in the high foxhouse window
where she was playing as a child; forty years
into adulthood and a master's degree from
Harvard have not persuaded Rinna that she
could have imagined this incident. My step-
daughters, both in college now, remain wary of
seeing Tayaĝunaax̂ when they are home for the
summer and out camping on the tundra. Not
that a college degree should confer truth or cast
doubt on the accounts of others—the *starosta's*,
for example, a church warden who saw
Tayaĝunaax̂ walk out of the sea onto Lukanin
Beach one evening. A devout and sober man, he
ran all the way into the village to the church
house, woke the priest, and begged to be blessed
with holy water. I have never seen Tayaĝunaax̂
though I believe he exists, on some level. Out
here among the animals, the Aleuts, and the
scientists, I have learned of the presence of
many things which, lacking my own or any
other's empirical evidence, nevertheless exist.

Still, when it comes to religion, I'm not so

easily convinced. Perhaps I should pay closer attention, but to what? The time my sweater caught on fire from a candle during the all-night Easter service, the most holy of Russian Orthodox ceremonies? Did I miss a greater meaning to the sudden flush of heat coming off my chest, the smell of hair burning, of Ernest slapping down the flames before I realized what had happened? It was a small fire as fires go and, other than a sideways glance from Ernest's wife and the roll of my husband's eyes heaven-ward, the service continued uninterrupted.

"I want to know God's thoughts," said Albert Einstein, "the rest are details." Einstein was a deeply spiritual man, though certainly not in any orthodox sense. He was profoundly engaged in the process of glimpsing greater truths, of examining, on many levels, "the marvelous structure of the existing world," and "the Reason that manifests itself in nature."

It is in this spirit that I stand both reflective and present during the hours of Sunday's Divine Liturgy; that I lie down in wonder beside the dead fox; that I listen again and again to the second movement of Dvorak's Serenade for Strings in E Major; and that I turn to watch the crushing pressure and sudden release that come with the most powerful storms.

The vernal equinox draws near and most of us going to work, to school, or to evening vespers will be unaware of the brief symmetry of daylight and darkness. The stillness outside persists. Few of us are in church this Lent, the weather is cold, and though I listen for the finch's song I have not heard it.

Field Notes

Two of the holi-
est people I've ever
known were here on
the island. One,
Father Sergius, came
from a ministry
serving about sev-
enty people in the
village of Old
Harbor on Kodiak Island. An Orthodox scholar,
linguist, and botanist, Father Sergius was born
in Caracas, Venezuela, and grew up in New
Jersey. As a young teenager he got on a bus
instead of going to school one day and went
north to a monastery. The monks returned him to
his family, but his pull toward that life
eventually led him to Mt. Athos, the holy
mountain of the Greek Orthodox Church, where he
lived and worked high above the Aegean Sea.
Then he came down from the mountain.

When Father Sergius arrived on St. Paul to
work with the community during our priest's

leave of absence, he embraced us with a warmth
and energy we had forgotten, blessed us with
his humor and curiosity, cooked and conversed
and walked with us. In the most profound way,
this man invited us back in: to ourselves, to
the island, and to the church. And just as he
uncovered historic manuscripts and vestments
stored and forgotten within the church, so he
seemed to help us find solace and promise
where we stood, with what we had, under whatever circumstances.

The church swelled with people attending
Divine Liturgy and vespers in numbers usually
found only at weddings and funerals; the line
grew so long for confession that it had to be
held earlier and earlier to accommodate those
comforted by his words, if not, through him,
by God's absolution. We did not fall under his
spell. He cast none except that of an ordinary
man caught by life as if by surprise, a surprise that was not temporal but sustainable.
In that way, he was extraordinary.

Father Sergius, a slender, bearded man with
a quiet voice, retained his monastic
lifestyle: he owned nothing, kept nothing—

though he was tempted, he once told me, to
hold on to some leather trousers his mother
sent him. He dressed in the black robes and
clothes the church gave him, cooked meals from
food donated to him, and it was rumored that
he slept on the only uncarpeted floor in the
church house so as to put as little as pos-
sible between himself and God. Among the
Pribilovians, where the acquisition of things
had come late—only within the last ten years—
and was still at full throttle, Father
Sergius's asceticism was striking. But it was
his full-hearted engagement with life, with
the taste of the morning and the tenor of the
birds and the condition of our souls, that
filled us, settled us, and excited us. And
when he left and rejected, without explana-
tion, our petition to the Bishop of Alaska
requesting his permanent placement on the
island, he taught us to carry these feelings
ourselves, to love not him, not even Him, I
think, but the landscape of knowledge itself.

Maxima Stepetin had a similar spirit, a
persistent rendezvous with the present. Honest
in all ways that mattered, he seemed free from

the constraints of public opinion after tragi-
cally losing his wife and children in a fire.
Maxima's face—triangular eyes, furrowed brow,
lower lip pulled down by scar tissue from the
fire—was full of humor and sadness as if he
himself had painted them there: broad, uneven
feelings too imposing to hide. But it wasn't
this that unnerved people as much as it was
the abandon with which he lived his life,
saying what he felt, doing what he wanted—
whether it was rowing alone eight miles out
and back to Otter Island or defying federal
regulations by killing seal pups for food in
broad daylight.

Maxima could be troublesome. During the
mid-1980s, when animal protectionists sent
"observers" out to the island to watch the
sealing as a form of protest, he would show up
on the killing field in his bloodstained
clothes, weaving a bit from beer, sharpening
his knives, and expressing a contempt toward
the visitors many of us felt but kept in
check. There was an edginess in all of us then
and many Aleuts seemed caught between anger,
frustration, and the need to not give the

activists more fuel for their fire. When it was suggested to Maxima that he wasn't helping an already tense situation by his presence, he waved off the charge with his trademark remark, "I don't give no never mind."

During the years I knew him, Maxima was usually in some state of inebriation and this, too, was not well regarded within the community. Like others, and for his own reasons, he was alcoholic; unlike some, he made no attempt to hide it. Yet those who dismissed him missed knowing a man who was also honorable, intelligent, self-deprecating, and generous. One summer when I was fishing commercially with my husband and working twenty-hour days, I mentioned in passing to Maxima that I hoped to get more organ meat from the seal harvest before it ended. When I came home the next day, he was sitting on my doorstep with a large plastic bag full of hearts and livers, prized meat he had himself taken from that day's harvest. He held fast to the traditional community ethic of providing for those who could not provide for themselves, often getting for elders fresh meat from the rookeries

or fish from someone's boat. And he possessed
an animal-like gentleness towards many people:
playful and kind, he could deflect suspicion
of any ulterior motives simply by his enthusiasm and determination.

Maxima was no sage but he was no fool
either, though he was sometimes treated as
one. What gave muscle to his life was his
endurance of all things, his fearless, uncompromising relationship with the land, the sea,
and the animals around him. Though he could
appear reckless he was, in fact, careful and
careless in all the right places.

Maxima died on a cold March night beneath a
black sky full of stars. He died freezing and
alone, filled with liquor drunk earlier that
evening to delight a group of partygoers who
wanted him to dress in women's clothes. Who
knows what went through their minds? Who knows
what corrupts one person but spares another so
that despite every indication and the appearance of foolishness there is, instead, an
uncommon decency and integrity?

Alaĝulix

To go into the sea

THERE IS NO PLACE on earth like the Bering Sea, no landscape that can be as seamless and harboring or as fractured and dissonant as this vast, high latitude stage. Out fishing on a still summer night under a high sun, the water a brilliant white sheet, the light and quiet as immense as a full orchestra, I have felt lost the way a child can be lost in play: completely, unaware of anything except the moss-like smell of the sea, the weight of a line in my hand, the presence of fulmars and kittiwakes settling nearby, and of seals surfacing. Climbing a rope ladder up the side of a factory trawler in the middle of the night with the winter wind gusting and the sea below black and primitive, I have felt fear run its course through me like lightning: electric, deadly, deliberate in its target. And between the calm and the storm I have enjoyed my time at sea even through hours of work so demanding I've not noticed the pitch of the boat or the condition of the sea itself.

For four summers I fished commercially, long-lining for halibut on the *Cleopatra*, a twenty-two-foot Oregon sea dory owned by my husband, Larry, and Ernest Stepetin. Later, I worked as an emergency medical technician with the St. Paul Search and Rescue team getting injured fishermen off ships. Exhilarating, exhausting, and sometimes terrifying, being on this different planet Ocean was like being in the run of a wild herd: moments of startling rhythm and a cadence so absolute that the distinction between who is who and what is what was lost altogether. Most of the time, though, I was reaching, turning, coiling rope, pulling gear, riding the run: fast, slow, up and down.

On occasions, when being on the water felt so familiar that I was no longer wary, the sea, like an animal sensing change, quickly brought me back to full attention: the wrenching force of a swift ocean current colliding with an opposing tide, somewhere deep beneath the boat, would vibrate up through the hull, through my feet, and shoot through my blood. I learned to pay attention every time, all the time. Each fishing season, twenty-foot swells loomed like falling mountain ranges, thick fog gave me vertigo, days without sleep left me wondering if it was morning or midnight. Everything changed: never sick at sea, I reeled around for hours on land, leaning against walls to steady myself.

I kept a log of our days out on the water, recording expenses, the amount of bait used, the number of fish caught, and the weight of each catch. Along with these were various observations: Ernest's unfailing patience and humor; the luminescence of a puffin's webbed feet and its long tufts, like streamers, celebrating flight; my shifting respect and resentment toward my husband as Captain. As the season progressed and weariness set in, my log entries were soon reduced to simple figures: the loran coordinates of a successful catch, the total weight and price paid us for each opening. On the boat, communication boiled down to look and gesture. On shore, our talk was pared to the bone: "Tea?" ... "Going for gas?" ... "Keys???"

Sometimes, windburned and worn out, Larry and I would lie in bed and roll cool oranges about our faces, settling them on our closed eyes, our cheeks, and temples. We would laugh at how ardently we had looked forward all year to these weeks of unrelenting stress. And then we would sleep for a few hours. I remember the dreams: of huge white fish with crescent-shaped tails dangling off our gear in the cold, dark water.

Half basin, half range, the Bering Sea is bordered east and west by Siberia and Alaska. To the north, through the narrow Bering Strait, lies the shallow Arctic Ocean; to the south, through the many passes of the Aleutian Islands, is the great Pacific Ocean, deepest in the world. And between them is the extraordinarily rich waterscape of the Bering Sea: site of fantastic bloomings of phytoplankton, the microscopic plants of the sea whose every cell is capable of converting light, carbon dioxide, and nutrients into the food upon which all other sea life depends; of zooplankton, tiny animals like copepods, crab, and fish larvae that graze across the sea's algae; of 450 species of fish, shellfish, and crustaceans—snails the size of fists, seven-inch arctic razor clams, and shrimp called pink, humpy, and coonstripe that spend part of their mature lives as males and the rest as females; of six species of seals, the Pacific walrus, and Stellar sea lion; of sixteen types of baleen and toothed whales and porpoises; and of fifty species of seabirds, waterfowl, shorebirds, and even raptors such as eagles and peregrine falcons. Along the coastline of this 885,000-square-mile sea are many human communities, most of them small, most made up of native people whose physical, material, and spiritual well-being depends on their traditional and evolving relationship with this body of water and the life it sustains.

In the southeastern Bering Sea is a distinct marine ecosystem of extremely high biological productivity that, each year, attracts extraordinary concentrations of fish, marine mammals, and seabirds. Their spring and early summer migrations transform Pribilof Island peninsulas, beaches, coves, cliffs, the sky above, and the sea itself into crowded, bustling territories. Here are breeding, nesting, and nursing animals who cannot forage long distances for food and depend entirely on what is available within fifteen to twenty-five nautical miles of the islands. To see the magnitude of life drawn to these shores and waters, to glimpse the complexity of the biological infrastructure supporting such life, is to see nature as a deeply conscious, greatly gifted architect, one of unsparing, unsentimental persuasion, a visionary, eclipsing all others.

The Pribilof marine ecosystem is unique in all the world's waters. It supports one of the Northern Hemisphere's largest seabird colonies and seal rookeries—several million birds and an estimated million northern fur seals—and vast populations of pollock, cod, flatfish, rockfish, other groundfish, and shellfish. Yet this is only the tip of the iceberg. Below, an immense network of interdependent life sustains, regulates, responds to, and is influenced by events occurring within its natural borders. Well-defined and specific compared to the rest of the sea in its hydrophysical, hydrochemical, and biological properties, this is the soul of a spectacular ecosystem.

It is also an ecosystem undergoing remarkable changes. For several decades steep declines have been documented in the number and reproduction rates of northern fur seals, harbor seals, Stellar sea lions, red-legged and black-legged kittiwakes, common and thick-billed murres, as well as various fish and shellfish stocks. These trends have been observed but their causes have not been understood. Considerable speculation has focused on a correlating period of intensive commercial fishing in the area. But the scope of an ecosystem is far larger and more complex than most of us realize. Vast fleets of fishing boats gobbling up millions of metric tons of the same food the animals depend on does not, unfortunately, tell the whole story or solve the mystery. Such exploitation may have a profound effect on the animals, but there are many other consequences and considerations: the effects of natural phenomena, both local and global, on the ecosystem; the combined effect of man-induced stresses with specific climatic and oceanic changes; and countless other equations, couplings and uncouplings, occurring in the middle and basic levels of this ecosystem. There has been comparatively little investigation into these regions, and without a comprehensive approach to understanding their minute and immense connections we are left with a deeply flawed foundation on which to build responsible-use and conservation policies.

Equally disturbing has been the tendency to marginalize, or ignore altogether, the observations of Native people about their environment. Aleut hunters and fishermen have long noted changes in the physiology and behavior of certain marine mammals and seabirds around the Pribilofs—thinning seal pelts, weak bird chicks falling off cliffs, killer whales attacking sea lions—signals significant enough in scope and occasion to leave the Aleuts concerned about some form of systemic food stress in the ocean. Yet, until recently, the information they passed on to the scientific community was regarded, at best, as anecdotal—random stories considered useless to the systematized methods of scientific research.

It is largely through the persistent efforts of a handful of Pribilovians, independent researchers, and a team of Russian research scientists that a broader, more integrated construct of investigation, conservation, and resource management has been pushed onto the table. In the early 1980s, researchers Susanne Swibold and Helen Corbett began what would become a long-term multidisciplinary partnership with the Pribilof Aleuts. At the time, their expansive approach to documenting and studying the events happening to the human and other animal populations on and around the Pribilof Islands contrasted sharply with mainstream western scientific inquiry, which was species, but not ecosystem, oriented; it did, however, complement the Native perspective of an interdependent world where no event is isolated in its influence. For the first time the Aleuts' knowledge about their environment was respected for its inherent scientific value, and the people themselves were recognized as an important link in the ecosystem's development. In retrospect, any other approach seems archaic, but it would take years to persuade the "official" world, where resource management decisions are made, otherwise.

Among the Pribilovians, too, there has been controversy over the value of various conservation proposals, particularly those that might affect their new reliance on the fishing industry. As St. Paul city manager, my husband brought environmental awareness into the development arena and was widely criticized by many villagers for his insistent efforts. Dubbed "Ecoman" by his opponents, Larry understood that the conservation movement which had emerged broadly in the American consciousness only in the last twenty years was offensive to his people's historical sense of stewardship and kinship with the natural world. Still, he argued, the principles were the same, that the evidence of food stress and declining animal populations demanded the Aleuts reinvent their traditional conservation ethic to address the contemporary situation.

There have been some successes. In 1992, the St. Paul City Council and the U.S. State

Department approved funding to bring over a team of Russian oceanographers and biologists with extensive experience in ecosystem-based marine research. Over the next three years Dr. Mikhail Flint and his team probed, sampled, and analyzed physical, chemical, and biological components of the Pribilof marine ecosystem. What they found gave scientists insight into the ecosystem's soul. It provided evidence of a distinct marine province that is both unusually productive and highly vulnerable.

Mikhail Flint is a tall, energetic man who grew up in middle Russia, where his family took him "deep into nature." His knowledge of the natural world has grown through a lifetime of exploration, research, and field work. Flint's enthusiasm unfolds when he speaks the precise, imagistic language of oceanology that is full of specific and interdependent meaning, of fric-tionless words that speak of a frontier most of us can only imagine. It is a frontier, Flint says, that needs our urgent, collective attention.

The very processes—such as water structure and intensive vertical mixing—which contribute to an environment of extreme biological productivity may also accelerate the transfer and incorporation of various pollutants into the ecosystem. The volume and types of pollution are wide-ranging: they come from the discharge of giant catcher-processing ships that house hundreds of workers and dump huge amounts of by-product wastes into the waters surrounding the Pribilofs; from the countless diesel fuel leaks and oil spills out of the hundreds of fishing boats and trawlers that anchor offshore during storms, that come and go for fuel, supplies, and to off-load catch and equipment; from the chemically treated waste produced by three large processing plants on the island, waste that is piped about a half-mile offshore; and by freshwater runoff from expanding, shore-based industrial areas choked with heavy equipment and activity like forty-ton Terex trucks that roar back and forth, day and night, for months at a time, between the St. Paul rock quarry and the harbor.

"We have an important psychological response to what we can actually see happening in an ecosystem," says Flint. "But it is critical that our response include a full understanding of the dynamics of the Pribilof marine ecosystem—on all levels: physical and chemical, biological, cultural, and economic." To ignore one component of any sphere of influence is like throwing dice and accepting whatever is won and lost in the play. But the stakes out here in this unique and magnificent marine ecosystem are so fantastic it seems improbable that anyone would risk the fate of its evolution with games of chance. Yet that is precisely what we've been doing.

There are obstacles to developing policies and programs that respond in substantive and sustainable ways to the Pribilof marine ecosystem: the highly vested interests of an enormously powerful and wealthy U.S. commercial fishing industry (56 percent of domestic fishery production comes from the Bering Sea); the conflicting directives of the Department of Commerce, which both regulates resource management in U.S. waters and encourages the development of ever more efficient fishing

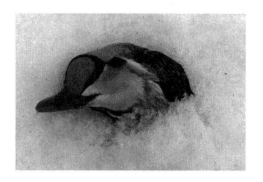

technology; the commercial whaling, sealing, and fishing interests of other nations such as Canada, Russia, Japan, Poland, Korea, Taiwan, and China; the depleted funding of environmental marine research; and the conflicting visions and hopes for the future of the Pribilof Aleuts themselves.

These facts have not discouraged those committed to changing the way we do business in the Bering Sea despite the recognition of a revenue-driven, ethically bankrupt system of policy-making. Larry has organized the Bering Sea Coalition, an alliance of coastal Natives increasingly influential in resource management. Swibold and Corbett, similarly convinced that a grassroots, regional approach is best, are actively engaged with the Aleuts on Russia's Commander Islands developing small-scale conservation economies. In Moscow, Mikhail Flint is drawing U.S. scientists and Alaska Natives into the ecosystem research fold by including their work and observations in publications detailing the most current comprehensive information on the Pribilof marine ecosystem. And some commercial fishers, as well as organizations like the Alaska Marine Conservation Council, are pushing responsible-use policies at local, state, and federal levels.

Together, these people are working to establish two international research centers, one on the Pribilofs and one on Russia's Commander Islands. These would provide the physical setting to encourage the integration of work being done by Aleuts and other indigenous people, by oceanographers, biologists, marine ecologists, ethnographers, naturalists, and artists from around the world.

We are fast losing our kinship with the natural world. The evidence is everywhere.

Walking Lukanin Beach north of the village
one March afternoon, I made a list of some of
the things I came across: engine gaskets in their
original Modesto, California plastic bag; fox
prints that suddenly stopped; a plastic dish-
washing detergent bottle; empty shotgun shells;
ash-colored driftwood—long poles, twisted
trunks, a huge wheel-shaped stump with sea-
bleached roots curving into air; pink and blue
foam padding; yards of tangled green fishing
net, and rope the color of bone; the top of a
yellow highlighter pen; a neoprene boot;
smooth basalt rocks, black as I approached,
indigo as I looked back; two plastic milk jugs;
and a dead king eider sea duck, deep vermilion
bill below a brilliant orange frontal shield, the
gray-blue crest on top of his head smoothed
back, and along the side of his still face, white
feathers turning the color of a pale sea.

Field Notes

     June 21. Summer solstice. Full moon.

     3 a.m. Twilight. Forty-seven degrees.

     Day off from fishing but not from work. Finished getting our gear ready a few hours ago. Four hundred hooks ready to be snapped on to over a half-mile of line, each hook baited and carefully coiled in baskets. Takes all my concentration to coil correctly. Of the many meticulous, sequential steps necessary for a successful catch, this is the only one that aggravates me. One misplaced hook snagging the line as it's running off the boat while we're setting our gear in the water will bring everything to a screeching halt: the boat, the line, our collective mood. By comparison, the physical labor of setting our gear and hauling it in is calming.

     Neon gave us a huge octopus for bait yesterday. It barely fit into the kitchen sink where I cut it up, all eight arms and that huge whitish head with two flat eyes I didn't want staring in my direction. I am tender-

hearted about octopi with their complex nervous systems, brilliant camouflaging, and clear intelligence.

Last week we caught a mottled orange octopus on one of our hooks. I wanted to throw it back into the sea. Larry and Ernest frowned. "Smart bait," Ernest said, eyes smiling. "We need it. To bring us good luck against the bad luck of having a woman on board." He laughed. Our hold was full of huge fish, twenty halibut, 838 pounds of fresh white meat that would net us over twelve hundred dollars for a ten-hour soak.

Being in a boat out at sea is like traveling in a dream: language can be troubling, birds fly underwater, landmarks aren't where you imagine, and you see, long before you hear, a killer whale's distant breach. Reverence—and terror—arrive suddenly or may build slowly. Gravity reveals a certain buoyancy. And the sea comes ashore with you: holding a cold fresh halibut steak above the stove, just before cooking it, feels like holding a block of deep ocean itself.

Once I wondered how fish experience pain. I called the chief fisheries scientist with the Alaska Department of Fish and Game, who supposed fish do "feel" pain but believed the concept of suffering was anthropomorphic and therefore not within the scope of reasonable discussion. A marine biologist with the University of Alaska's Center for Fisheries and Ocean Sciences said he'd thought about this question a great deal but could draw no conclusions. Fish, clearly, are wired differently than humans. The neurological structure of their brains does not include, among other features, a limbic system which in mammals is where the experience of pain and similar events are initially registered. Yet fish, like humans, release measurable amounts of hormones when subjected to even mild stress. They also demonstrate a visible, violent biological response to unpleasant stimulus— being hooked, for example. But is this just a primitive, instinctive reaction, the "flight or fight" response that man defines as un- conscious, mechanical behavior?

Finally, I called Bill Rogers, trusted friend, fisherman, and chief of emergency medicine at one of the country's largest hospitals. Bottom line, Bill said, since fish avoid pain they obviously "experience" it in some way. The set point for how it is experi- enced depends not only on the species but also on the environment. "Someone who lives in Beverly Hills and flies first class feels pain differently than someone who lives on the street." In any event, Bill pointed out, fish are unavailable for comment, so we'll never know.

Hippoglossus stenolepis, Pacific halibut, are the largest of all flatfishes. Most that we catch weigh between 50 and 150 pounds, but a St. George fisherman brought in a 398-pound fish yesterday. Must have been around a long time. Females can live over forty years, males almost thirty years. Young halibut living in water columns have eyes on each side of their heads. As they grow and become bottom-dwelling fish, the left eye migrates to the right side of the fish so that they have both eyes on the upper side of their bodies. Nature is endlessly clever; halibut moving along the ocean floor need to focus most of their attention above. Their color adaptation is smart, too, camouflaging them from predator and prey. The upper side of the fish is dark and tends to assume the colors and mottled appearance of the ocean floor. The underside is white, sky-like if seen from below.

4:30 a.m. The sun's rising light burns up from the sea.

Foxes are down on the boats picking at fish guts and bait. Timon's new boat is clearing the breakwater. Simeon and his crew are already setting gear out past Southwest Point. Beyond them, a gray band of fog stretches east to west as far as I can see. The marine fore-

cast is for winds north-northwest from five to
ten knots, increasing to twenty knots by
tonight. Seas five feet building to eight
feet. Fog and drizzle. The only place I've
lived where the fog is so thick a steady wind
doesn't blow it away.

Asxi-lix

To go against the wind

O NE MORNING I watched from a distance as a group of men quietly walked into a rookery full of northern fur seals and dark volcanic rocks bordering the sea. A thin white fog hung over us and the air had that stillness in which all sound and scenery seem diffuse. I could hear the men's voices, their whistling and the clapping of hands as they began circling the seals, moving them across Zapadni Cove toward the killing field. I could hear the seals' movement, flippers and fur, across the ground. Within minutes, heat was rising off their backs like storm clouds.

About thirty of us had turned out to help with the subsistence seal harvest. Waiting in the tall grass near the rookery, we leaned against our trucks, sharpened knives, and talked about sealing, fishing, the weather, local politics, and our families, catching up on news as we seldom get to during the brief summer months. Every once in a while I looked up to watch the seals slowly moving toward us. As they got closer, the harvest manager, Richard Zacharof, began organizing the field, choosing the most experienced men for the most critical jobs, all of which require strength and skill: "stunners" who kill the seals with a swift club on the head; "stickers" who puncture each seal's heart; "rippers" who attach huge steel-ribbed implements to the skin of the dead seals and then, two men to a carcass, pull off the pelt; and "meat cutters" who carve the carcasses.

Each year there seem to be fewer experienced sealers, men who know how to do the job well or how to do it with the same measure of pride and respect as their elders. Until the mid-

1980s when the U.S. government stopped its for-profit operation on St. Paul, sealing had been the only economy on the Pribilofs. There had been a certain honor among the Aleuts, a sense of traditional tribal ethics at work in the way they went about their work; there had been a feeling of identity—"my father and his father and his father were sealers for the Americans and Russians"; and there had been pride, "my ancestors subsisted on seals and other Bering Sea marine life for thousands of years."

In 1984, mounting public criticism flamed by a provocative, often inaccurate media blitz led by the Humane Society of the United States prompted the federal government to end its commercial sealing operation on St. Paul. A trust fund was established to help the Pribilovians' economic transition from a wholly government-subsidized industry to private development.

Still, the transition was abrupt. Aleut leaders had few of the skills needed to run a remote village dependent on air and marine transportation. With soaring fuel, oil, and electrical costs and no economic base, the eight hundred men, women, and children on the Pribilofs faced a crisis. Courted by oil companies and the fishing industry, and concerned with the growing tension in their small communities, the Pribilovians mapped out a future. The ensuing years of rapid development and social upheaval have sometimes taxed the islanders' individual and collective reserves. And sealing, for so long a central part of the Aleut culture, is no longer only a customary gathering to harvest traditional food. It has become a proving ground: Outsiders will not take away the Pribilovians' right to kill seals for food.

Back in the field, after an hour of herding, Steve Melovidov and his crew had moved the seals up onto the far edge of the killing field. Five boys were stationed around the perimeter of the herd to keep any animals from escaping. Richard and Steve talked, looking over the seals, while Macrina Zacharof went over the list of orders from villagers: how many seals each family had requested, who wanted whole carcasses, who wanted the "butterfly cut," who wanted flippers to pickle for *lastax̂*, who wanted the highly prized hearts and livers to make *agan uma qanox*, a favorite dish. Other field workers unrolled huge sheets of plastic bags, separated them, and placed them along one edge of the field to collect the fresh meat as it was cut. Those of us who had come to cut our own meat picked up some bags, helped where we could, and then moved out of the way to wait for the harvest to begin.

Vlass Shabolin stood next to me, shaking his head and gesturing toward a pickup truck full of teenagers and loud music. "They shouldn't do that," he said. "Used to be kids would never do that around sealing." He remembered the old days of the commercial harvest when the sealers were up and out on the rookeries before dawn and the government's quota of killing twenty to eighty thousand seals a summer kept villagers busy for weeks on end. He remembered when the work was back-breaking, the days endless, and fresh seal meat was the only decent food the Aleuts were given to eat. Vlass shook his head again, "Now some of the young kids don't even like it."

From the other end of the field a half-dozen seals were culled from the large group and herded toward the stunners who eyed them carefully. Only two-to-four-year-old male seals, too young to breed, are killed in the subsistence harvest; pups, older males, and females are released to make their way back to the rookery. When the lead stunner was ready, he signaled the others. Each man took aim with a long wooden club, quickly delivering a fatal blow to each seal. These animals were pulled back a few yards, their hearts pierced, and the skin cut around the neck, fore and hind flippers. While one group of men separated another small pod of live seals from the herd and moved them toward the stunners, other workers began pulling off pelts and cutting up carcasses.

A young blond woman in a shiny green slicker standing near me put her hand over her mouth and started backing away from the field. She had flown out to St. Paul to meet her boyfriend, whose fishing boat was docked in our harbor for a few days, and she had hitched a ride out to this morning's harvest. "This is not what I expected," she said, turning away.

There is nothing gentle about killing animals for food, whether pulling a twenty-five-year-old halibut from the sea by hook and gaff, slamming a cow on the head in a slaughterhouse, or slitting a pig's throat. It is bloody, messy, up-to-your-elbows work. People either do it themselves—typically, indigenous people like the Pribilovians, subsistence farmers, and hunters—or have others do it for them. And those accustomed to picking up their meat in the supermarket are often appalled by the act of killing. We forget that the clean, cellophane-wrapped packages of beef, pork, lamb, chicken, and fish come from the carcasses of once living animals. I was not surprised by the young woman's shock.

A total of sixty seals were killed that July morning. Richard and Steve helped me cut up five carcasses, about half the seal meat Larry and I used each winter and spring. The harvest crew worked past noon in the field, trucked the bags of fresh seal meat back to the village, and delivered them to people's homes. I spent the rest of the day slicing the dark, protein-rich meat from the bones, dividing ribs, soaking hearts and livers, and packaging everything carefully for the freezer. It is not easy labor, processing meat from field to freezer, and those who taught me how to do it have impressed me with their diligence and their determination not to waste anything they've worked hard to put by for their families. This is a practical conse- quence of subsistence living as much as it is a cultural ethic. It is also one of those ironic twists of nature, a pact of respect that binds the killer to the killed, the hunter to the prey, in ways difficult for the uninitiated to understand. Yet most of the people I know who exist, par- tially or wholly, from subsistence have a deep appreciation for the animals they eat and the environment that supports them.

As I worked in my kitchen that day I real- ized it was the first time in nine years that the Aleuts had conducted their subsistence seal harvest without actual or threatened interference from the Humane Society of the United States (HSUS) and other groups such as Friends of Animals. Over the years I had come to feel that these people's objection to killing seals for food, under whatever legal language or ethical posturing, had more to do with their own fragile, removed understanding of life and death than it had to do with a reasoned response to saving marine mammals. Unable to claim that killing sixteen hundred non-breeding seals a year threatened the health of the whole herd, HSUS worked to influence federal regulations governing the subsistence seal harvest, to focus the National Marine Fisheries Service on "percent-use" (the average percentage of meat and bone removed from the carcass, by weight) as an indicator of waste. This proved controversial and, ultimately, ineffective: percent-use values were highly suggestible figures on paper but did not indicate any real waste on the killing field. While other highly respected organizations such as the National Audubon Society consistently supported the Pribilovians' subsistence harvest, HSUS forced the Aleuts for years, at great legal expense, to defend their right to take seals for food. At best, their effort to end or further limit subsistence sealing can be seen as misguided. At worst, it speaks to a kind of cultural arrogance that should not be tolerated.

In the Smithsonian publication *Perceptions of Animals in American Culture*, the authors define the many attitudes from which we humans view animals: naturalistic, ecologistic, moralistic, humanistic, and utilitarian to name a few. They note that whatever our individual prevailing attitudes, we humans tend only to speak out about the ethical treatment of "preferred animals"—seals, dolphins, and others that appeal to us for one reason or another. They conclude that no single system of dealing with animals exists that would appease the varied concerns of the public. But they write that we "must avoid the polarizing righteous indignation that does not respect the human values and concerns of those with different views." The Pribilovians, who to this day must conduct their subsistence harvest under the only on-site federal observation program in the country, would agree.

Animals have died and will continue to die for our sustenance, our comfort, and our vanity. We are often unaware of the animal products we use every day. For leather belts, cosmetics, watch straps, and the canned food we feed our pets, animals have been killed. And what of our own preferred foods? The fish we eat may have been caught in massive trawl nets that indiscriminately maim and kill hundreds of thousands of "bycatch" animals every year: pups, pregnant and nursing females, breeding males. Such deaths are not restricted to seals, of course, but include sea lions, dolphins, whales, sea otters, common and rare seabirds, and countless other species of marine mammals.

The killing of domesticated animals—horses, cows, pigs, and chickens—is no less violent, their pain no less felt, than the seals killed on St. Paul. Should we then consider the quality of life of domesticated animals? Those headed for the market are often raised under cruel conditions, sometimes force fed, some-

times mutilated, and frequently injected
with drugs to make them produce more and
taste better.

"The whole of nature," observed theologian
William Ralph Inge, "is a conjugation of the
verb to eat, in the active and the passive." Most
of the thousands of northern fur seal pups born
on the Pribilof Islands each year do not survive.
They are killed through disease and starvation,
eaten by sea lions and orcas, strangled and
drowned by discarded fishing nets and other
debris filling our oceans. These are some of the
true stories in nature, of predator metamor-
phosed to prey. They are ancient narratives
reenacted each day in every sea, across the
arctic and subarctic tundra, across the great
plains, the deserts, through mountain ranges,
rolling hills, in city parks, and suburban back-
yards. We may not see them, may not choose to
see them, but our aversion does not belie reality.

The killing fields of St. Paul Island, with
their thick foliage fertilized by the blood of
seals across the centuries, stand in marked

contrast to the island's other grasslands. On each of them, I have held the still-warm heart of a wild animal in the palm of my hand. It is both an unsettling and privileged thing to have done.

Field Notes

Late July 6.

7 a.m. Misting. About forty-eight degrees.

My stepdaughter, Marissa, and I are packed into the room-size cab of a pickup truck with biologists, students, an Australian journalist, and Terry Spraeker, who has been the federally mandated "humane observer" of the seal harvest for years. We are on our way to the Reef Point seal rookeries. Marissa has been working with the seal biologists all summer and this morning will help with dead pup counts. This involves walking onto the breeding grounds, climbing the scaffolding that runs about eight feet above the seals, and inching along two narrow, slippery planks running the length of the rookery. Dead seal pups are picked up from below with a long pole and noose, put in a sack, and taken back to the lab for necropsies. The cause of death is added to other research components aimed at understanding the dynamics of the fur seal herd. I am along because it's the closest I

can get to breeding seals. Life out on the
rookeries is astonishing.

"We used to think we should bring a gun
along on the catwalks," Spraeker says. "So if
you fell off and into the seals you could just
shoot yourself. It would be a lot quicker and
less painful than being ripped apart by the
bulls." Spraeker laughs but he's serious.
Moving into an active breeding seal rookery is
invading the territory of many large, fierce
animals. Mature bull seals can weigh up to six
hundred pounds. Several months of fasting,
breeding, and defending their territory leaves
the bulls easily provoked. The female seals,
either nursing, sleeping, or making their way

through other harems to feed at sea, are smaller but equally captious. Nor would a person want to quarrel with a seal pup, twenty to sixty pounds of hungry youngsterhood equipped with needle-sharp teeth. In a word, they are wild.

Marissa, utterly fearless about life in general, presses up against me as we weave our way toward the rookery. Spraeker, a few steps ahead, stops periodically to negotiate his way past a bull. Holding a long pole in his hands like a tightrope walker, his demeanor is determined but not confrontational. The bulls snort, bark, bear their canine teeth and shake their heads at us, and let us pass. Stop and go. We have split from the rest of the group to come out to this distant rookery. It is taking awhile for the three of us to make our way through the increasing number of seals, the rocks, and slick mud. As we approach the catwalk ladder two large bulls sit like sentinels on either side. They are in no hurry to move away. We stop again. This time I breathe deeply, pulling myself up to a moment filled with the rolling sounds of seals and the sea, of

Marissa's presence, and my own heart beating.

Spraeker moves toward the bulls, adjusts the pole in his hands, says something fierce I can't quite catch. The two seals move a few feet toward the rookery and within a minute we are up on the catwalk crawling just above the densely packed breeding ground. Each harem is marked by a large brown bull's presence and an unruly but definable group of females and pups. It's a busy, noisy place where almost every seal—and there are thousands along this stretch of shore—seems fully involved: the males flashing eyes, teeth, and warnings at us as well as toward other bulls; the silver and dun-colored females negotiating hungry pups, belligerent bulls, and the varied moods of other *maatkax̂s*; the wet black *laaqdax̂s,* seal pups, engaging each other, their mothers, and anything else they encounter as they move about the rookery.

Spraeker and Marissa work the length of the catwalk while I lie still on my stomach gradually focusing on individual seals. I am struck by many things as I watch these animals: the harshness of their environment,

the tenacity of their hold on life, the
immensity of that moment when a *maatkax̂* calls
for and finds—or does not find—her own pup.
But it is the distinct behavior of the male
and female seals that most captures my
interest. Their movements and language suggest
the base instincts, urges, and actions of our
own behavior—behavior barely masked by recent
evolution. The successful mature male seals
have managed for months to hold their ground
and their females by brute force and constant
wariness; covered with infected cuts and open
wounds they seem as much victim as master,
driven by the deep, deliberate nature of their
biology. The female seals appear fierce,
frequently annoyed, not particularly maternal,
with a marked "emotional" intelligence that
effectively communicates their busy schedules:
alternately nipping or lashing out at males
six to ten times their size and weight, for
example, as they head out to feed. Aware that
my own biases further influence such
anthropomorphic observations, the gender-
specific behavior of the seals nevertheless
seems a profound reminder of our not-so-distant

connection to each other: species to species,
male to female, animal to animal.

A pup has caught sight of me and looks up
with filmy black eyes, nose twitching, body
curving, hind flippers scratching his coat in
a losing battle against fleas. Irritating
bugs, empty stomachs, cut flippers, preoccupied or absent mothers. Marissa is back. She
sits a few feet from me, watching, long legs
dangling off the catwalk.

Qutaxt

Blowing up from land

O NCE I WRAPPED the skull and antlers of a large reindeer in cardboard and cloth. It took me an hour to pad the thirty-four points of the rack but only a few minutes to pull an old bed sheet snugly around the long head and tape it up. When I was finished the antlers looked comical with odd bits of cardboard pointing in every direction. But the skull, broad at the forehead, tapering down with perfect symmetry to the nose—the skull, wrapped in pale cloth, held my attention. Several large raindrops pooled on the end of it, and in the gray midday light the skull seemed to symbolize the permanence of beauty and the persistence of form. Against my objections, my husband was taking the rack to friends in Canada.

We had come across it on a hike to Crater Hill earlier that fall. The cone of this old volcano rises from the widest part of the island and is a two-hour hike from the nearest road. The actual distance is not great but the terrain is difficult: elbow-high grass covering a maze of slippery tussocks and wide, bony mats of rocks punctuated by deep holes. When we got to the volcano we climbed up and over the break in the crater and found the lake bed dry. Larry went down to explore while I headed up the spine of the cone's steep ridge. To my left, the earth fell away in dry rubble and scoria; to my right, thick grasses and wildflowers carpeted the crater's interior.

The wind was strong that day and I see-sawed back and forth along the ridge as I made my way up, dipping into the warmth of the interior, pushing back up into the cold, sharp

wind. A short way from the top I saw the reindeer skull and antlers. Caught by the hard rock
scrabble, the rack faced northeast, the direction
from which we had come. I imagined it following our progress from the road, the wind
through its antlers the only comment on our
coming. It seemed an unusual place for a reindeer to have died and I wondered how the head
and antlers had come to rest upright in such an
exposed place, on such unsteady ground. I
circled the rack, crouched behind it to see what
it might see, and photographed it from many
different angles. But I did not touch it and I left
it there.

The ridge of the cone peaked and evened
out about five hundred feet up. I walked along
the rim until I came to a small boulder which,
oddly, roughly, seemed to point skyward.
Behind it, protected from the wind, was one
small flower, a wild blue flax. I sat near it, my
back against the boulder, and looked down the
slope of grass and wildflowers to the lake bed.
My husband was down there eating his lunch. I
shouted to him but my voice rose and flew back

across the ridge with the wind.

Several hours later, we met at the base of the volcano. The reindeer rack was lying at Larry's feet. I was startled and angry. I felt it should have been left where it was, but he thought otherwise: "It's meant as a gift for Susanne." Then he turned and walked away, raising the skull and antlers over his own head and lowering them onto his shoulders and back. The rack seemed to fit perfectly there, as if my husband had been somehow incomplete all these years without it. Together they formed a striking image, this man with huge white antlers reaching skyward like lightning, like an archangel fallen to earth, his wings stripped of their feathers. I watched him weaving through the tall grass, singing. And I watched him carefully from every angle over the next few hours as we made our way back to the road. Not an archangel, I concluded. Reindeerman.

Like a story, every walk has a beginning, a middle, and an end. With the rack all packed up, my husband's business trip took him first to Oklahoma for a conference, then to Canada to visit our friends Susanne Swibold and Helen Corbett. The skull and antlers proved difficult to carry: they wouldn't fit into any rental cars, not even into a trunk with the hatch left open, and were refused at airport storage areas. Airline ticket agents who, in Anchorage and Seattle, are used to Alaskans transporting all sorts of odd things, were hesitant about checking the rack through as luggage or freight. Canadian customs officials balked at it, insisted it was a caribou, and wanted to know if my husband had a hunting license. "No," he replied, fastening his dark eyes on them. "The reindeer belong to our people." On the drive from Calgary to Banff the car lost traction and hit a guard rail.

Small acts of resistance, I thought. Part of the journey, said my husband.

Susanne put the reindeer skull and antlers on a votive pole on her property in the foothills of Canada's Rocky Mountains. It is a place of honor. She is a woman of integrity. Still, it seems a miscalculation. I often look at the photograph of the reindeer rack as I came across it on the island that day: the huge, wide antlers a ballet of bones beneath the sky— movement, caught and stilled.

The wild reindeer on St. Paul are wary of humans and hard to get near with their excellent sense of smell and tendency to walk into the wind. They bunch up as one herd most of the winter but separate during calving in the spring. I came across dozens of does and their newborn calves one clear April day, warming themselves on a southern slope near the sea. They didn't acknowledge my presence, so I stayed for a long while listening to the soft coughing sounds the mothers occasionally made to their young. I'd read that these are the only species of deer in which both males and females grow antlers. Some biologists believe this indicates the does assume a higher rank in the herd after the bucks shed their antlers, and that each calf born shares its mother's place in the herd's hierarchy. Reindeer antlers are not only indicators of inheritance and social structure, they are also amazing vehicles of metabolism. They grow like other bones by forming cells but these cells grow at an astonishing pace, faster than any other type of living tissue except that of a developing embryo. Doctors have likened this aggressive growth rate to cells found in malignant bone cancer and are interested in the mechanism controlling such growth.

Reindeer were brought to the island in 1911 as part of a state-sponsored program relocating small herds of these arctic deer from Siberia to northern and western Alaska where caribou did not roam in winter. The government thought the animals might prove a source of fresh meat through the cold months, although the Aleuts had traditionally eaten sea lion, harbor seal, and duck during winter. The reindeer were well suited to island life: willing to eat seaweed and drink seawater, able to survive on lichen during the winter, they also thrived on the tundra's lush vegetation during the summer and fall. But the government failed to manage the herd and by the late 1930s two thousand reindeer roamed the island, overgrazing the tundra.

Some village elders remember their parents' stories about the time the herd was too large and hundreds of disoriented, starving reindeer fell off the headlands. What remained of the herd was slaughtered during World War II by the government and another herd was introduced in the 1950s.

"We used to eat a lot of reindeer," my *kruusnaⱡ* (godmother) once told me, remembering the roundups carefully planned by villagers each fall. But the meat changed, "too wild," after the new herd was brought up from the Aleutian Chain. There are no longer any formal roundups on the island. The tribal government, which now manages the herd, kills about forty deer each year for community subsistence and another forty or so animals are taken by individual hunters with permits. But the herd has grown in recent years, once again leading to concern that the tundra is being overgrazed. This was brought to the community's attention largely by elders out berry-picking each August. In a village this size, it only takes a handful of women going to their sons and daughters and announcing, "No berries again this year. Reindeer are eating them all," before some action is taken. Last year, the tribal government began culling the herd. The carcasses are cut up for meat and sausage, the hides sent north to a Shishmaref tannery, and the antlers are sold or kept for crafts.

Once I came across several hundred reindeer trapped in a slough between a few well-placed hunters. Circling in on themselves, the animals in the center of this hurricane-like motion were turning slowly, almost leisurely, as if unaware of any threat while the deer galloping around the outside seemed frantic, a tangled, moving mass of bodies, heat, and hooves. Eventually a large buck broke free. I watched his long gait as he headed across the open tundra, watched as he dropped mid-stride, his antlers catching in the grass, his huge head following, tumbling under his chest, under his body until it, too, came round with startling force. Suddenly he was still, his long body and pale hide blending, bleeding into the tundra, the buck himself dead before I even heard the rifle shot. The herd faltered, as if one animal, then continued across the slope until it disappeared in a cloud of snow and antlers.

Wild animals in winter give life to the windburned carapace that covers the island for so many months. And whereas reindeer make themselves scarce, the ubiquitous arctic fox feels free to walk right by children, cats, and cars to rummage through our garbage bins when the going gets tough. Though physically small, arctic foxes are adaptable, fearless, and curious. They tend to command our respect. I had viewed them with a certain amount of affection until the day one appeared out of the January fog and walked right up to me. Standing less than a foot away, this dark little creature peered up at me as I peered down at him, examining his fine triangular face, his eyes diffusing and reflecting the light like two perfect oval pools. Friends here had warned me never to look into the eyes of a fox. "He'll steal your soul," they said. I remembered this advice after several long minutes of intimate, mutual examination when I realized neither of us was

moving away. I stood up, hooted at the fox, shooing him away with my arms. He wasn't impressed, stepping back just a few feet as he kept his glassy eyes fixed on mine. I stomped toward him in my big winter boots. He stood his ground. I stomped and shooed and hooted. He turned and trotted away, glancing back several times, his face dark again, the light gone from his eyes. For days after this encounter I felt uneasy, as if I had brushed up against some unrecognizable force.

Aleuts have long believed foxes are tricksters of sorts, capable of being inhabited by spirits. There is the story of "Foxwife," a woman who left the village long ago to search for her husband after he failed to return from hunting. The woman found she was ill-equipped to deal with the terrain and weather and so changed herself into a fox. But she never found her husband and some villagers say when a fox looks into and locks onto your eyes it is Foxwife searching for her mate, hoping to take your soul. Other stories and warnings about foxes are less metaphysical. Parents still warn their wandering children never to follow foxes and, for emphasis, point to the cross on a bluff above the graveyard. It marks the spot where a young boy fell off the cliff to his death after following a fox along the ridge.

Foxes may first have come to the Pribilofs by ice. The southern edge of the arctic ice pack reaches down to the islands every few years and foxes are known to travel considerable distances in their search for food: one intrepid animal found along the coast of northern Alaska had been tagged along the coast of Russia the year before. Often foxes will follow a polar bear across the ice pack, feeding on the remains of seals killed by the bear. Polar bears have even come ashore here: the remains of three have been found in various places on the island, including one of the caves in the dormant Bogoslof Crater in the middle of the island. The last polar bear known to have traveled this far south walked onto Northeast Point in the winter of 1920 and was shot by a villager.

One of the abiding images I have of wildlife in winter here is that of a fox sitting on the edge of a high bluff, her small dark body profiled against an ocean flashing with light, ears forward, eyes scanning the sea and sky. Though I turn and walk away, back toward the clutter of human life, the fox's form burns in my eyes the way a bright light will if you look at it then close your eyes. I try to imagine the fox's thoughts, her hunger, what she is smelling, how her feet feel against the earth, how it feels when the air stirs her fur. I imagine what it must be like to live completely in the present. I want to slip beneath her coat, feel a muscle in my back stretch as I reach down to sniff, prick my ear back to recognize a sound, feel the sharpness of a bird's fine bone against my gum as I bite into it, taste the food as it slides down my throat. Am I full? Or am I still hungry? What do I see when I dream?

It is a futile exercise, of course. Integrating my understanding of animals—from the pets I grew up with to the grouse and deer I hunted in New England to the seals, fish, and birds I have butchered out here—brings me no closer to experiencing life as they do. I will never know all the creatures or their languages, never know even one creature, this fox, and its language. Realizing this doesn't stop me from trying. I've read books on animal cognition, talked to friends in the village about their experiences, listened to stories, watched animals for hours on end, studied their carcasses. Still, the fox exists for me as a creature translated by human thought, word, and emotion.

I talked about this one afternoon with a friend in the village. He shook his head, said I was spending too much time alone, that only an *amerkanch*—slang for white person—would worry over such thoughts. Animals just *are*, he told me, and the only way to be with them, to experience anything similar to what they might experience, is to spend a great deal of time in their environment. "If you can do that long enough, the animal will teach you about his world. But that's as close as you can get."

When I was young, a man taught me to move as quietly as a deer through every season in the forest. It took years of non-practice, emptying myself of that certain human consciousness, my senses turning more on the instincts of predator and prey, my awareness settling into muscle, tissue, breathing, and silence. By the time I had learned the Zen of deer hunting, my life was changing course in other ways and I moved across the country to San Francisco. Still, I have always known the experience was one of the more important ones in my life if for no other reason than the occasional yielding up of a self that was polished clean of thought. "There is nothing more animal-like," writes the poet Wislawa Szymborska, "than a clear conscience/On the third planet of the Sun."

Muscle, tissue, breathing, and silence.

Bone, skull, and antlers. Silence.

Field Notes

Midnight.

Couldn't sleep. Drove out along the Reef Point headlands. The light was electric, the ocean shadow-blue, the curve of the planet drawn across a broad, open horizon and marked by the dark band of color where the sky absorbed the sea. Walked along a worn path near the bird cliffs and listened to the percussive barking of bull seals, the nattering of *maatkax̂s,* and bleating of pups.

Restless. Unwilling to let summer go. Stood against the wind on a bluff and watched the kittiwakes and fulmars coast on the currents. Saw a dark, distant cormorant bending her long neck to her breast. The white nights are over.

Everywhere, here, the landscape and life it supports is changing, realigning itself to move as the sun moves, north to south, to cross the celestial equator. It is late August, a time of harvest and celebration at lower latitudes. A calendar above my desk notes the telling names various Native Ameri-

can tribes give this month's moon: Big Ripen-
ing Moon (Creek), Seals Fattening Moon
(Penobscot), Moon of the New Corn (Cherokee).

Up here in the subarctic sea, summer's
harvesting of seals, fish, bird eggs, sea
urchins, putchkii, and moss berries is over.
The lupines, which for weeks hung like a blue
haze just above the grasses, are brown, each
flower pod bulging with seeds like a chrysalis
soon to release a butterfly. Other flowers
like the purple monkshood and arctic poppy are
holding their color, the petals tearing
slightly, wearing in the fall winds.

The tundra is turning yellow, flashing like
waves of gold under the sky's dark backdrop,
pale again in the bright sun. The light seems

temperamental: one moment black, the next moment blinding. I, too, am volatile. During confession at church I confess my irritation with the visiting priest, confess that I don't believe fear, guilt, and intimidation are the appropriate chords to strike in his instruction of religion. Do you want people to come to church like sheep herded to the edge of a cliff?

All around the outermost reaches of the island on the black sand beaches and basalt rocks the seal harems are breaking up, the huge, gaunt bulls returning to the sea to eat and drink for the first time in months. The female seals are fattening their pups, nursing, sleeping, and feeding for days out at sea. The pups, thousands of small, plump *laaqudax̂,* are gathering in loose nurseries scratching, biting, climbing, and standing around on young flippers staring at life from ground zero. Out on the high bluffs tens of thousands of summer birds are preparing to head for their winter grounds, their nests coming apart, the fledglings falling, tumbling down cliffs, dying, or flying.

The luminous summer sheet of fog and sun
that has blanketed us in stillness for months
has lifted, has left, and in its leaving
pulled up the cold air from the sea and
spilled it over us.

Qag, Agaagalix̂

East wind, west wind

THE SUN HAS EMERGED in a pool of blue sky after weeks of storms. When I have been worn down by constant wind, the sudden stillness and light are like coming up for air after a long dive: astonishing, disorienting. We are on the other side of winter but far from spring and it is this stretch between seasons that seems longest to me. The Aleuts used to call this period The Time for Eating Thongs, the time when their food supplies started to run out, the great fish had yet to return, and storms made it hard to get out on the sea and hunt for food.

I am hungry for the warmth of the sun and the smell of new plants pushing through the earth. I am irritable, too, barking at the moon and at my mate, scratching at winter's steel door, wanting out. But it will be many months before the wildflowers bloom and the *laaqudux̂*—the seal pups—are born. Many months before we are out during the white nights of summer, walking the tundra, listening to the island's quiet interior, startled to find it is midnight.

I call this period Time to Travel Outside. An Alaskan colloquialism, Outside, always capitalized, is a word that succinctly states the mind-set of most who live inside this state: that this is it, the most awesome place on earth to live, and any place beyond its borders is simply Outside—beyond, amorphous, obscure. It's not meant to be arrogant, only to convey the deep, often inexplicable love affair people have with this state.

Still, most of us non-Alaska Natives originally come from Outside. We have family

Outside, people who love and miss us and sometimes wish we'd come "home." If we live in the Bush, many relatives and friends really wish we'd come home. Yet few people are able to leave Alaska forever once they've lived there, and even fewer leave who've tasted life in the Bush. What seems unimaginable to others—living, for instance, on a small island with one store, one gas pump, and twenty-something miles of unpaved road—becomes the only way we want to live.

"What do you *do* up there?" my brother, a lawyer in Boston, asks periodically. It's difficult to say, to translate for someone the power of weather and wildlife and how they can fill up your day, how most every day is filled with the routine and the remarkable, the routine as perplexing as figuring out dinner, the remarkable as extraordinary as watching thousands of birds leave the island in one great, long flight from the headlands.

Flying east from the Pribilofs to Anchorage takes two and a half hours on an old Reeve

Aleutian Electrajet. We all joke about "Reeve
Aleutian, The Final Solution" but our confi-
dence in this airline, its pilots, and the planes is
absolute. We've watched from inside the cabin
or from the ground as Reeve negotiates sudden
50-mph crosswinds or near-zero visibility to
land on St. Paul's rough airstrip. We've hedged
our bets on Mike Z.'s ability to orient an in-
coming pilot by radio, from his truck on the
runway, under the most severe conditions.
We've entrusted the most precious cargo, our
children, to entire planeloads in their ritual
flights to and from the island and boarding
school. We've bumped and rattled and prayed
our way through winter storms and summer fog
and we've been safe.

On board, after months on the island, the
transition to Outside is somehow eased by the
steady drone of four Rolls Royce turbo-prop
engines. The passengers, all of whom generally
know each other, talk back and forth across the
seats and aisles or drift back into silence, read,
and sleep. Crises happen. A woman, on her way
to Anchorage for medical treatment, has a heart

attack a half-hour out of St. Paul. We do CPR,
ask the pilot to divert to Dillingham, feel her
die beneath our hands, hold her daughter close
for the rest of the flight. On another flight,
Northern Air Cargo allows Piama to ride home
in the jump seat. She is bringing her uncle's
body from Anchorage back to the island for a
late afternoon funeral. The plane develops
mechanical problems and diverts to Bethel.
Hours into the repairs and still on board, Piama
finds a mattress in the hold, puts it on top of
Yayitop's casket, lies down on it, and falls
asleep. When the plane eventually arrives on St.
Paul she says the funeral will have to wait until
the next day. "Yayitop and I are too tired for
that today," she explains to her seven children
and everyone goes home.

Anchorage, a stepping-stone in my two-day
trip to the East Coast. The city is a flat, sprawl-
ing intersection—a paved, hazardous point of
connection between the Bush and Outside, a
place of arrivals, departures, shopping malls,
towering oil company headquarters, littered

vacant lots, and architecturally dazzling Native corporation buildings.

The next day, flying low over Seattle, it's impossible not to see the true lay of the land beneath the concrete and patchwork yards, to imagine how extraordinarily beautiful this peninsula must have been just a few hundred years ago: rolling hills and high plateaus covered with long grasses, ancient trees, bluffs sloping down to calm coves, and only the sound of wind, birds, and the language of thought. At the airport, with a four-hour layover, I walk outside: it's raining, green, busy. Back inside, travelers are straining toward a television set in a bar. Something about the Unibomber threatening to blow up a plane out of Los Angeles. I ask the airline personnel where the plane I'm about to board originated from that morning. Los Angeles. How do I gauge such a threat? Carefully, I decide, since human dementia is as unpredictable as weather. No one is helpful, least of all the airline, though I eventually persuade them to give me a seat on a different plane. Another stepping-stone on which the briefest pause turns precarious.

Up in the air again, heading east over and past the Rockies. The land below flattens, rises, erodes; there is space everywhere, hundreds of miles of everything but the trappings of humans. By the time we are over the Midwest, the terrain is marked in giant, unfathomably precise transections so straight, so square it's hard to believe someone didn't reach down from the sky with a pencil and ruler and map it all out for the farmers. The farms gradually give way to suburbs, cities, and highways glinting like steel ribbons through the haze. Between Chicago and Washington the ground is gathered up and plaited like some geological accordion.

Yet Washington, D.C. is in full spring bloom, a city of fresh greenery, trees, flowers, bushes, parks, and the great silver swath of the Potomac sliding towards the Atlantic. Sitting on my mother's porch I am surrounded by the sweet, sweet smell of honeysuckle and of earth warmed by the sun. Pansies, a friend says, lost their fragrance when the gods found field workers lying around intoxicated by the

flowers' perfume. Zap. The scent was removed. Work resumed. *Les pensées sauvage*
somehow survived their loss of redolence and
thrive today in my mother's garden, gray-blue
clouds gathering across the ground, ready to
spill their story if we could hear the words or
read the signs.

When I was here last, it was August. I had
come for the thunderstorms, the thick air, and
the sound of cicadas through the night—things
I missed after ten years in Alaska. Day after day,
I sat on the porch soaking in the humidity until
I was a furnace: full, hot, and still. But April is
August's counterpoint, the air cool, fluid, full of
light and colors. Animal life is everywhere: pale
butterflies, big, slow bumblebees, brown and
black squirrels, Canada geese, grackles, wood-
peckers, crows, familiar dogs and cats, and, at
night, opossums and raccoons out back. Each
time I visit I am amazed at the wildlife in the
city, at the close quarters we share.

Alaska can be a curious calling card, like
saying you're from Cameroon, or Pluto.
People are interested in the weather, the

landscape, the wildlife, whether it's dark all winter and light all summer. Then comes that sticky question: "What do you do up there?" Sometimes I'm asked if I feel any culture shock when I come east. I don't—which either makes me mindless or mindful, depending on your thinking. For all the dissimilarities between island and city life, for all the unique, defining elements—from geography to language—that distinguish the Pribilofs, there are fundamental consequences of modern life common to all environments. Visionary leaders, inspired artists, selfless teachers—promise, hope, despair, poverty, crime, opportunity, and pollution—the Pribilofs have it all, albeit in closer quarters. In a more remote setting. Without any traffic lights.

Many urban visitors to St. Paul have remarked, with astonishment, that the island is a microcosm of their world. They are often surprised to find such intense political divisiveness, to learn about the tangle of international regulations, the federal and state hoops we jump through just to work traditional fishing grounds. Surprised to see that fax machines, Patagonia® jackets, and Ford Explorers® are as much a part of the landscape as freshly butchered seal meat, weary fishermen, and children playing spirit games. For many outsiders, Alaska is a mythical country with a few white cities, a big oil field, lots of wild animals, and isolated Native people who fashion arts and crafts.

On my mother's porch the light changes. Dark clouds move in like rush hour traffic. I listen to the air, the birds, and watch a colony of orange ants filing back and forth from the garden to the grass. My mother and father are intrepid travelers and have visited St. Paul many times. They share my appreciation of life there and if they wish I'd come home they don't mention it. They are full of questions about the people they know, about the latest news, the rumors, and whether I intend to continue this "hair-raising" adventure of search and rescue work.

In Boston, visiting my brother, it's another matter altogether. He has still not forgiven me for moving so far away, still can't understand what it is I do there. Up where he is, on the eighteenth floor of One International Place, Eric is embracing, disarming, remarkably focused in the most distracting of atmospheres. His clients include autistic children, the sexually abused, the mentally ill, people who have been wronged by the system, the church, by their own biochemistry, or some deranged individual. We talk about a new case he's working on, his defense of a brilliant man whose recently publicized unorthodox views have greatly disturbed the institution where he works. We talk about Eric's two lovely young daughters, about his wife Margot juggling motherhood, architectural clients, and a fulltime college teaching position. He wants to know when I am coming home and we laugh because it has always been this way between us: difficult, admiring, confrontational about each other's lives. Later, he introduces me to some colleagues. "This is my sister Sumner from Alaska," he says, as if Alaska was my last name.

Flying west, homeward. Between Boston and Seattle, the other passengers will all be strangers. Between Seattle and Anchorage, about twenty of us will know each other. On Reeve Aleutian's flight from Anchorage to St. Paul, I'll know every person on the plane. I'll find out if Marfa has had her baby, Tuilipop his surgery, how the Seattle-based crabber *Aleutian Enterprise* sank in less than five minutes on calm seas, and if the police chief is going to stay another year.

Field Notes

Then there are
the cats.

Pud, Agripinna,
and Polovina, born
under porch steps,
thrown out after
kittenhood, or

taken to the dump to die picking through the
frozen garbage. A friend said he's counted sixty
cats out there. They do not go of their own
accord: the dump is far from the village.

Driving back from Northeast Point one day I
saw a flash of white in the tall grass near the
road. I stopped, backed up, watched a long-
haired white and orange cat slip down the road
toward the volcano called Polovina, watched her
stop and stare at me. We were eight miles from
the village. I knew the cat, knew the family the
cat claimed. For an hour, the cat and I assessed
each other, me trying to gain her trust, she
caught between trust and fear. Or was it love and
hate, need and independence? She would not come

143

close enough. She had been there long enough
that wariness was curving into wildness. I drove
back to the village, got seal meat and a big
cardboard box, and drove back to find Polovina.
Already I had named her for the place where she
was abandoned.

Polovina lived between our houses, Sugar's
and mine. God must have been considering cats
when He moved me in next to Sugar Owens. Sugar is
catlike herself—fine, fierce, quick, and giving
with eyes the color of smoke. For years we made
temporary and sometimes permanent places for the
cats between our lives, our affection for them
spilling out into boxes with towels and scraps
of food and money we didn't have spent on long
distance phone calls to an Anchorage vet, plane
tickets for the suffering but salvageable cats
we could not bear to kill. We watched over them
and, as importantly, watched out for them. One
morning I saw Sugar glaring at a group of young
boys glaring back at her. Her arms, across her
chest, suddenly flew open and she said, preda-
tory, possessive, protective, "If I ever catch
you hurting any cats again I'll rip your ears off."

Another time, coming back from the airport, I

saw a thin black tangle of hair wandering between the caged towers of stored crab pots. I
stopped and the cat, a Persian I knew, came
toward me dazed, half-dead, but smelling empa-
thy. I picked her up gently, little more than
bones and fur, reeking from starvation and
infection. Her voice was broken, but I felt her
cracked purring on my thighs as I drove home. I
sent her into the Anchorage vet clinic when she
was stronger. She cast magic on the employees,
who willed her to live, but she died a week after
arriving. Later, I confronted the people who, a
year before, had shown off their prize Persian
cat as if she were furniture you could not sit
on: expensive, pedigreed, and rare. The man, who
I knew and worked with, said: "We couldn't keep
her after the baby came. Nothing's going to keep
my son awake at night." The cat was thrown out of
the house.

How to make a case for cats out here where
wild animals are dying in polluted seas and
people are struggling to survive? How to make
a case for cats when the deadline is past and
our children, adored and neglected, are playing outside long into the night?

Chax̂atax̂

An offshore wind

TO LIVE ON THIS treeless island in the Bering Sea is to live between broad sheets of water and sky, to become accustomed to open space, and to forces—wind, ice, tides—wiping out what is peripheral, rootless, impossible. Here I learned to leave alone dying seal pups stranded on remote beaches, to turn from arguments confined to hard ruts in the road, to get outside in order to make loose change of whatever was going on inside.

Landscape and geography open and close us in unexpected ways. A friend who lives surrounded by trees imagines she would feel too exposed living in such open space. But exposure becomes a kind of shelter: from the crowded territory of self, the uneasy navigation of relationships, the persistent inventory of truth and doubt. So it happened that by the time the air twisted between us every time Larry and I spoke, my response was to leave the house, drive into the storm, to the hill above the breakwater, the wind's glancing blows shaking the truck, shaking me, but oh, there—look! The long, long draw of a surging wave backhanded by the breakwater, gathering my disquiet in its fold, in its full foaming breath for one final pass, the swell rearing, arching, roaring across the rampart, slamming down across the docks and down across the harbor ships moving like nervous horses in a corral.

What sustains us, connects us, keeps a very few of us bound together, bloodied but never failing each other, never walking away? Larry and I had weathered ten years together when

we decided to separate. The dislocation felt
extraordinary as I left the island with our young
son. Yet what has proven as remarkable is how
connected Ian and I remain to the island, to
family and friends living there. Beyond the
frequent telephone calls, the summer visits, the
exchanges of all kinds, there is a sense of still
belonging to the community, of an inseparable,
common citizenship that we have not been
asked to forfeit in taking up residence else-
where. This is a large, gracious gesture, to be
welcomed home each summer with *peruga* and
alladiks by my mother-in-law, with a greeting in
church from Father George, and in conversa-
tions with elders. The general indifference to
our presence reassures us that we are unexcep-
tional, familiar parts of the whole.

Ian Alexander, at five, slips determinedly
from the affectionate embraces of his *kookax̂*,
his beloved sisters, *kruusnax̂* Piama, the strong
arms of his father. "Let me goooo," he says,
racing off only to return and engage each in a
mock battle or conspiracy of some glorious
kind. Aware of having to fly "day and night" to

get to the island, Ian's world remains bound-less: geographic, political, and cultural borders are not yet drawn on his map.

Each summer I feel again the irreducible energy and dignity in the wildness of nature, the wild and separate peace I have come to know on this island. It is a changeless and changing landscape. The harbor is busier and more built upon every year, new housing cuts across the tundra, the kids I first knew as children are wrestling with adulthood, further difficulties are born from existing ones, and many of the political divisions and environmental crises are as acute as ever. The white nights of summer still leave me sleepless. And the storms, great winds streaking the sea with ribbons of life, of energy from far away, still draw me to the beach with their lucent darkness and diamond light. But now a young hand holds mine.

Back in the house, my son dances and tosses a white cloth in the air, over and over, up and down, twirling, collapsing, reaching, turning, running until, shot through with joy, he says, "I am Wind."

Further Reading

The Pribilof Islands have proved a magnet for biologists, ethnographers, geologists, historians, marine ecologists, naturalists, oceanographers, ornithologists, and a wide range of research scientists, writers, and others during the last two hundred and fifty years. As a result, dozens of books and hundreds of articles, papers, and the like have been published. I have listed some of these for readers interested in a broader understanding of the islands than my own brief sketch ever intended. This list is informal, necessarily brief, and reflects my own access to such publications. As such it is incomplete but hopefully suggests the volume of material available. Also included are the works of various authors whose poetry or prose, though not always directly related to the Pribilofs, nevertheless deepened my own appreciation for life in the Bering Sea. My grateful acknowledgement to all of them, and to the many *Unangan*, Aleuts, whose stories are folded within these pages.

Aleut Dictionary, Unangan Tunudgusii, compiled by Knut Bergsland (Alaska Native Language Center, University of Alaska Fairbanks, 1994).

Alexander, Fred, M. D., "Medical Survey of the Aleutian Islands (1948)," *The New England Journal of Medicine*, vol. 240, no. 26 (1949).

Baker, Ralph C., Ford Wilke, and C. Howard Baltzo, *The Northern Fur Seal*, Circular 336 (United States Department of the Interior, 1970).

Black, Lydia T., *Social Transition in the North, Ethnographic Summary: The Aleutian-Pribilof Islands*

Region, Working Papers, vol. 1, no. 3 (Social Research Institute, 1993).

Brodsky, Joseph, *So Forth* (Farrar, Straus and Giroux, 1996).

Carson, Rachel, *The Sea Around Us* (Oxford University Press, 1951).

Chernov, Tu I., *The Living Tundra* (Cambridge University Press, 1985. Izdatel'stov "Msyl" 1980).

Dall, W. H., "Is Alaska A Paying Investment?" *Harper's New Monthly Magazine*, vol. 44, no. 260 (1872): 252-257.

de Groot, Rudolf S., *A Functional Ecosystem Evaluation Method as a Tool in Environmental Planning and Decision Making* (Nature Conservation Department, Agricultural University, Wageningen, The Netherlands, 1986).

Desmond, Alice Curtis, *The Sea Cats* (MacMillan Company, 1944).

Dragoo, Donald E., Belinda K. Bain, Arthur L. Scowls, and Rosalind F. Chaundy, *Status of Cliff Nesting Seabirds in the Pribilof Islands, Alaska, 1976-1988: A Summary* (Alaska Maritime National Wildlife Refuge, U.S. Fish and Wildlife Service, 1989).

Dumond, Don E., *The Eskimos and Aleuts* (Thames and Hudson, Ltd., 1977).

Dushkin, Augusta, Sophia Pletnikoff, Anfesia Shapsnikoff, Agnes Sovoroff, Sergie Sovoroff, Annie Tcheripanoff, and Bill Tcheripanoff, *Unugukulux Tunusangin, Oldtime Stories*, edited by Ray Hudson (Ounalashka Corporation, Unalaska City School District, 1992).

Elliott, Henry W., *Our Arctic Province: Alaska and the Seal Islands* (Charles Scribner's Sons, 1887).

Elliott, Henry W., *Report on Seal Islands of Alaska* (United States Department of the Treasury, Special Agents Division, 1884).

Fagan, Brian M., *The Great Journey: The Peopling of Ancient America* (Thames and Hudson Ltd., 1987).

Final Conservation Plan for the Northern Fur Seal (Callorhinus ursinus) (National Marine Fisheries Service, 1993).

Fiscus, Clifford H., Hiroshi Kajimura, and Gary A. Baines, *Pelagic Fur Seal Investigations, Alaska Waters, Special Scientific Reports—Fisheries No. 475 (1962), Fisheries No. 489 (1963) and Fisheries No. 522 (1964)* (Bureau of Commercial Fisheries, Fish and Wildlife Service, United States Department of the Interior, 1964-65).

Ford, Corey, *Where the Sea Breaks Its Back* (Little, Brown and Company, 1966).

Fur Seal Flippers and Other Delicacies: The Aleut People of St. Paul Island Cookbook (Alaska's Child in association with Wrangell Publishing, 1985).

Golovkin, Dr. Alexander N. *Colonial Seabirds of the Pribilof Islands, Analysis of Environmental Problems in the Surrounding Area, Final Report*, All-Union Research Institute of Nature Conservation and Reserves (Moscow, City of St. Paul: AlaskaBering Sea Publishers, 1991).

Griffin, Donald R., *Animal Minds* (The University of Chicago Press, 1992).

Griffin, Donald R., *Animal Thinking* (Harvard University Press, 1984).

Gsovski, Dr. Vladimir, Chief of the Foreign Law Section, Law Library of the Library of Congress, *Russian Administration of Alaska and the Status of the Alaska Natives* (United States Printing Office, 1950).

Investigation of the Pribilof Marine Ecosystem: Reports to the United States Department of State and the City of St. Paul, Alaska. Golovkin, A. N., Flint, M.V., Merculieff, I. P., et al., Vol. 1 (1993): 257. Flint, M.V., Drits, A.V., Emelianov, M. V., et al., vol. 1 & 2 (1994): 504. Flint, M.V., Drits, A.V., Emelianov, M. V., et al., vol. 1 & 2 (1996): 665. (P. P. Shirshov Institute of Oceanology: Moscow. City of St. Paul, Alaska).

Islands of the Seals: The Pribilofs (The Alaska Geographic Society, 1982).

John, Betty, *Libby: The Alaska Diaries of Libby Beaman* (Houghton Mifflin Company, 1987).

Jones, J. B., "Environmental Impact of Trawling on the Seabed: A Review," *New Zealand Journal of Marine and Freshwater Research*, vol. 26 (1992): 59-67.

Jordan, David Starr, *Matka and Kotik* (The Whitaker & Ray Company, 1897).

Kipling, Rudyard, "The White Seal," from *The Jungle Book* (1894).

Laughlin, William S., *Aleuts: Survivors of the Bering Land Bridge* (Holt, Rinehart and Winston, Inc., 1980).

Martin, Fredericka A., *The Sea Bears* (Chilton Company Book Division, 1960).

McCartney, Allen P., *Prehistory of the Aleutian Region*, Handbook of North American Indians: Arctic, vol. 5 (Smithsonian Institution Press, 1984): 119-135.

Mousalimas, *The Divine in Nature: Animism or Panentheism?* (University of Helsinki, 1990).

Munroe, Kirk, *The Fur Seal's Tooth* (Harper and Brothers, 1898).

Oleska, Very Reverend Archpriest Michael J., *The Alaskan Orthodox Mission and Cosmic Christianity* (Juneau, Alaska: St. Nicholas Orthodox Church, 1994).

Oliver, Mary, *House of Light* (Beacon Press, 1990).

Perceptions of Animals in American Culture, edited by R. J. Hoage (Smithsonian Institution Press, 1984).

The Romance of the Alaska Fur Seal (Fouke Fur Company, 1958).

Scheffer, Victor B., *The Year of the Seal* (Charles Scribner's Sons, 1972).

Stanton, Stephen Berrien, *The Bering Sea Dispute* (School of Political Science, Columbia College, 1887).

The Story of the Pribilof Fur Seals (United States Department of Commerce, 1976).

Swibold, Susanne, *Bering Sea Restoration Plan, A Summary* (Amiq Institute, Cranmore, Alberta, Canada, 1992).

Szymborska, Wislawa, *Sounds, Feelings, Thoughts: Seventy Poems* (Princeton University Press, 1981).

Terrey, Barbara Boyle, *Slaves of the Harvest* (Tanadgusix Corporation, 1978).

Unangam Ungiikangin kayux Tunusangin, Unangam Uniikangis ama Tunuzangis, Aleut Tales and Narratives Collected 1909-1919 by Waldemar Jochelson, edited by Knut Bergsland and Moses L. Dirks (Alaska Native Language Center, University of Alaska Fairbanks, 1990).

Williams, Gerald O., *The Bering Sea Fur Seal Dispute* (Alaska Maritime Publications, 1984).

Author's Note

Further information on the programs mentioned in this book may be obtained from:

Amiq Institute
276 Three Sisters Drive
Cranmore, Alberta T1O 2M7 Canada
Phone (403) 678-5027
Fax (403) 678-2879

Bering Sea Coalition
Box 149
St. Paul Island, AK 99660
Phone (907) 546-3190
Fax (907) 546-2573

Pribilof Marine Ecosystem Research Program
P. P. Shirshov Institute of Oceanology
Russian Academy of Sciences
Krasikova Street 23
Moscow, 117851, Russia
Phone (095) 124-7749
Fax (095) 124-5983

ARCTIC
CIRCLE

R U S S I A
(SIBERIA)

B e r i n g

KAMCHATKA POLUOSTROV

KOMANDORSHIYE OSTROVA
(Russia)

Petropavlovsk Kamchatskiy

A L E U T I A N

Attu I.

Kiska I.

P a c i f i c   O c e a n